ROAD MAPS *for* THE PSALMS

For a copy of Road Maps for The Psalms please send a donation to *The Master's Academy International*, 24307 Magic Mountain Parkway #540, Valencia, CA 91355-3402. All donations will help *The Master's Academy International* support ministry training centers and send biblically sound training materials all over the world.

The Master's Academy International provides resources and materials to train men to effectively proclaim the Word of God. Along with this, TMAI presents you with ways to maximize your effort in world evangelism and international missions. Join in the advance of the kingdom of our Lord Jesus Christ, to the glory of God!

The Master's Academy International
24307 Magic Mountain Parkway #540
Valencia, CA 91355-3402
661-295-6232
www.tmainternational.org

ROAD MAPS *for* THE PSALMS

Inductive Preaching Outlines Based on the Hebrew Text

GEORGE ZEMEK

*This volume is dedicated to all of the servants
ministering around the world under the umbrella
of The Master's Academy International.*

2 Timothy 2:2

From the Author

I am indebted to Dr. Paul R. Fink,
my 'father' in inductive-descriptive-parallel sermonic
outlining based upon Hebrew and Greek texts of Scripture.
By God's grace and enablement, you also have many
'grandchildren' and 'great grandchildren'
in the "method."

2 Timothy 2:2, 15; 3 John 4

Psalm 1

By two cycles of contrast Psalm 1 separates all people into their respective spiritual camps.

1A. By observation all people are *separated ethically. (vv. 1-4)*
    1B. A picture of the godly *(vv. 1-3)*
        1C. Their inclinations: *(vv. 1-2)*
            1D. described negatively *(v. 1)*
            2D. described positively *(v. 2)*
        2C. Their illustration *(v. 3)*
    2B. A picture of the ungodly
        1C. Their inclinations *(v. 4a)*
        2C. Their illustration *(v. 4b)*
2A. By outcome all people are *separated judicially. (vv. 5-6)*
    1B. The failure of ungodly people *(v. 5)*
    2B. The fruition of godly and ungodly lifestyles: *(v. 6)*
        1C. recognition *(v. 6a)*
        2C. ruin *(v. 6b)*

Psalm 2

Psalm 2 progressively shines its poetic spotlight on four vivid scenes relating to the mutiny of mankind.

1A. In scene one the poetic spotlight falls upon mankind *exposing human rebellion.(vv. 1-3)*
   1B. Their anarchy *(v. 1)*
   2B. Their arrogance *(v. 2)*
   3B. Their announcement *(v. 3)*
2A. In scene two the poetic spotlight is raised up to God *expressing divine reaction.(vv. 4-6)*
   1B. His amusement *(v. 4)*
   2B. His anger *(v. 5)*
   3B. His announcement *(v. 6)*
3A. In scene three the poetic spotlight swings to God's Mediator *establishing divine rule. (vv. 7-9)*
   1B. His position *(v. 7)*
   2B. His possessions *(v. 8)*
   3B. His power *(v. 9)*
4A. In scene four the poetic spotlight drops back down to mankind *exhorting human responsibility (i.e. Repentance is the only antidote for rebellion). (vv. 10-12)*
   1B. The demands stated *(vv. 10-12c)*

Note that there are five commands which may be grouped into two logical categories of obligation:

   1C. Wise up! *(v. 10)*
   2C. Worship! *(vv. 11-12c)*
   2B. The dependency solicited *(v. 12d)*

Psalm 3

'A Pattern for Praise, Peace and Prayer amidst Pressure'
Note the superscription (i.e. the Psalm heading or title)

Through three interrelated historical phenomena David shares with us his theological 'secret' of having assurance in the face of adversity.

1A. The psalmist's *predicament (vv. 1-2)*

    1B. The panoramic picture of his predicament *(v. 1a)*

    2B. The progressive picture of his predicament *(vv. 1b-2)*

        1C. The swelling ranks of his enemies *(v. 1b)*

        2C. The slandering rhetoric of his enemies *(v. 2)*

2A. The psalmist's *peace (vv. 3-6)*

    1B. Developed from Divine precedents: *(vv. 3-4)*

        1C. God's Person induces peace *(v. 3)*

        2C. God's provisions induce peace *(v. 4)*

            1D. The appropriation of His provisions *(v. 4a)*

            2D. The confirmation of His provisions *(v. 4b)*

    2B. Documented by personal practice: *(vv. 5-6)*

        1C. the habit of past practice *(v. 5)*

            1D. Its affirmation

            2D. Its explanation

        2C. the hope for future practice *(v. 6)*

3A. The psalmist's *prayer (vv. 7-8)*

    1B. Its individual focus *(v. 7a)*

    2B. Its undergirding foundations: *(vv. 7b-8a)*

        1C. God administers retribution *(v. 7b, c)*

        2C. God authors rescue *(v. 8a)*

    3B. Its corporate focus *(v. 8b)*

Psalm 4

'Rest in Peace'

At the end of yet another day of pressure, pain, and persecution, David engages in three mental contexts of conversation which ultimately lead to a point of blessed relaxation.

1A. He *prays to God* for preservation. *(v. 1)*
    1B. His request
    2B. His remembrance
    3B. His restatement
2A. He *reasons with his enemies* about repentance. *(vv. 2-5)*
    1B. He exposes their need of repentance. *(vv. 2-3)*
        1C. Through their fabrication *(v. 2a)*
        2C. Through their futility *(v. 2b)*
        3C. Through their frustration *(v. 3)*
    2B. He exhorts them to pursue repentance: *(vv. 4-5)*
        1C. concerning me, change your attitude *(v. 4)*
        2C. concerning God, change your approach *(v. 5)*
3A. He *praises God* for true perspective. *(vv. 6-8)*
    1B. A true perspective is defined by contrasting outlooks: *(vv. 6-7)*
        1C. the testimony of the skeptics *(v. 6)*
        2C. the testimony of the satisfied *(v. 7)*
    2B. A true perspective is demonstrated by a contented outcome. *(v. 8)*

Psalm 5

'Help Me and Harm Them!!'

David bases his respective prayers for Divine intervention and imprecation upon two rounds of contrast which differentiate the enemies of God from the children of God.

1A. Round one: David's *prayer for intervention* is based upon a theological contrast of retribution with reconciliation. *(vv. 1-8)*

    1B. David's prayer for intervention is expressed. *(vv. 1-3)*

        1C. Its passion *(vv. 1-2a)*

        2C. Its persistence *(v. 2b)*

        3C. Its promise *(v. 3)*

    2B. David's prayer for intervention is explained. *(vv. 4-8)*

        1C. God's enemies will experience retribution. *(vv. 4-6)*

            1D. Negative affirmations develop God's retribution. *(vv. 4- 5a)*

                1E. Affirmations about Character *(v. 4)*

                2E. An affirmation about consequence *(v. 5a)*

            2D. Positive affirmations depict God's retribution. *(vv. 5b-6)*

                1E. God despises His enemies *(v. 5b)*

                2E. God damns His enemies *(v. 6a)*

                3E. God detests His enemies *(v. 6b)*

        2C. God's children experience reconciliation. *(vv. 7-8)*

            1D. As evidenced by a desire for liturgical worship *(v. 7)*

            2D. As evidenced by a desire for lifestyle worship *(v. 8)*

2A. Round two: David's *prayer of imprecation* is based upon a practical contrast of the wayward with the worshipful. *(vv. 9-12)*

    1B. David's prayer of imprecation is expressed *(vv. 10 a, b, c)*

        1C. * 'Expose' Your enemies! *(v. 10a)*

        2C. Entrap Your enemies! *(v. 10b)*

        3C. * 'Expel' Your enemies! *(v. 10c)*

*Note Kidner's usage herein of the descriptive terms 'exposure' 'collapse' and 'expulsion.'

2B. David's prayer of imprecation is explained. *(vv. 9, 10d-12)*

    1C. God's enemies are wayward. *(vv. 9, 10d)*

        1D. Samples of their waywardness *(v. 9)*

        2D. A summary of their waywardness *(v. 10d)*

    2C. God's children are worshipful. *(vv. 11-12)*

        1D. Fitting expressions for worship *(v. 11)*

        2D. Foundational explanations of worship *(v. 12)*

Psalm 6

As we listen to David's cries coming from the depths of his personal pit of persecution, we are able to detect a radical change in his frame of mind as he addresses two different audiences.

1A. In the process of pouring out his soul before God we detect *a defeatist frame of mind. (vv. 1-7)*

    1B. His requests convey a tone of helplessness. *(vv. 1-4)*

        1C. Avert your anger. *(v. 1)*

        2C. Anoint my being. *(v. 2)*

        3C. Acknowledge my plight. *(v. 3)*

        4C. Administer your deliverance. *(v .4)*

    2B. His reasonings confirm a tone of hopelessness. *(vv. 5-7)*

        1C. My public worship will cease if I die in these circumstances. *(v. 5)*

        2C. My personal weariness will consume me if I live under these circumstances. *(v. 6-7)*

            1D. From weeping *(v. 6)*

            2D. From waning *(v. 7)*

2A. In the process of turning his attention to his enemies we detect *a defiant frame of mind. (vv. 8-10)*

    1B. His boldness conveys this defiant frame of mind. *(v. 8a)*

    2B. His basis confirms this defiant frame of mind. *(vv. 8b-10)*

        1C. His confidence in answered prayer returns to him. *(vv. 8b-9)*

        2C. His confidence in anticipated payback refreshes him. *(v. 10)*

Psalm 7

'Surviving Slander'

We are able to detect spiritual advancement in David by following him attitudinally through three progressively calming stages of expression in response to the painfully false accusations that were being hurled at him.

1A. Stage one: ***David's concern*** as he passionately begs the attention of the Divine Judge *(vv. 1-5)*
    1B. Via his cause *(vv. 1-2)*
        1C. His precedent for Divine attention *(v. 1a)*
        2C. His pleas for Divine attention *(v. 1b)*
        3C. His pressure for Divine attention *(v. 2)*
    2B. Via his curse *(vv. 3-5)*
        1C. The conditions of this curse *(vv. 3-4)*
        2C. The calamities of this curse *(v. 5)*

2A. Stage two: ***David's court*** as he painstakingly argues his case before the Divine Judge *(vv. 6-16)*
    1B. He begins his day in court by focusing upon the Just Judge's relationship with the righteous. *(vv. 6-10)*
        1C. This is the basis for his explicit requests for a judgment in his favor. *(v. 6)*
        2C. This is the basis for his general summons to convene the trial. *(vv. 7-8a)*
        3C. This is the basis for his personal invitation to scrutinize the actions and motivations of both parties. *(vv. 8b-10)*

        Notice his invitations to 'begin with me first' (v. 8b)

2B. He continues his day in court by focusing upon the Just Judge's relationship with the unrighteous. *(vv. 11-16)*

    1C. The character of the Divine Judge should sober them. *(v. 11)*

    2C. The ultimatum related to the Divine Judge should shake them. *(vv. 12-13)*

    3C. The sentences of the Divine Judge should scare them. *(vv. 14-16)*

Note the principle of lex talionis in these sentences.

3A. Stage three: ***David's composure*** as he patiently waits for the verdict of the Divine Judge *(v. 17)*

Psalm 8

'Praise from the Puny'

The beginning and concluding bursts of praise in Psalm 8 are driven by David's contemplation of two pairs of radical contrast.

Introductory Praise *(v. 1)*
    Its corporate expression *(v. 1a)*
    Its individual expression *(v. 1b)*

1A. The first pair: A radical *contrast between the nature of 'infants' and infidels (v. 2)*
    1B. Explicitly, through the affirmation of 'infants' *(v. 2a)*
    2B. Implicitly, through the autonomy of infidels *(v. 2b)*

    Note the NT's Messianic application of these principles in Matthew 12:15-16.

2A. The second pair: A radical *contrast between unaided general revelation and unveiled special revelation (vv. 3-8)*
    1B. The yield of unaided general revelation: Man is puny within the expanse of God's creation. *(vv. 3-4)*
        1C. David's contemplation *(v. 3)*
        2C. David's conclusion *(v. 4)*
    2B. The yield of unveiled special revelation: Man is prominent over the expanse of God's creation. *(vv. 5-8)*
        1C. The dignity of man's prominence *(v. 5)*
        2C. The delegation due to man's prominence *(vv. 6-8)*
            1D. The bestowal of his dominion *(v. 6)*
            2D. The breadth of his dominion *(vv. 7-8)*

    Note the NT Messianic development of Adam theology
    in 1 Corinthians 15:27 and Hebrews 2:6-8.

Concluding Praise *(v. 9)*

Psalm 9

David's hymn in Psalm 9 ebbs and flows through two respective tides of praise and prayer.

1A. The first tide is one of ***Divine justice and praise.*** *(vv. 1-12)*
    1B. Individual praise and Divine justice *(vv. 1-4)*
        1C. The giving of it *(vv. 1-2)*
        2C. The grounds of it: *(vv. 3-4)*
            1D. via David's assurance *(v. 3)*
            2D. via David's affirmation *(v. 4)*
    2B. Divine justice and corporate praise *(vv. 5-12)*

Note the inverse order: praise (vv. 1-2), grounds (vv. 3-4);
grounds (vv. 5-10), praise (vv. 11-12)

        1C. The grounds of it: *(vv. 5-10)*
            1D. the Judge's dealings with godless men *(vv. 5-6)*
            2D. the Judge's dealings with all men *(vv. 7-8)*
            3D. the Judge's dealings with godly men *(vv. 9-10)*
        2C. The giving of it: *(vv. 11-12)*
            1D. via the community's affirmation *(v. 11)*
            2D. via the community's assurance *(v. 12)*
2A. The second tide is one of ***Divine justice and prayer.*** *(vv. 13-20)*
    1B. Individual prayer and Divine justice *(vv. 13-16)*
        1C. The giving of it *(vv. 13-14)*
        2C. The grounds of it: *(vv. 15-16)*
            1D. with a focus on depravity *(v. 15)*
            2D. with a focus on Divinity *(v. 16)*
    2B. Divine justice and corporate prayer *(vv. 17-20)*

Again, note the inverse order.

1C. The grounds of it: *(vv. 17-18)*

      1D. in conjunction with the godless *(v. 17)*

      2D. in conjunction with the godly *(v. 18)*

2C. The giving of it *(vv. 19-20)*

Psalm 10

'Hope Dawns for the Hopeless'

The psalmist's voiced expressions in Psalm 10 exemplify how true believers seem to live in two different worlds at the same time.

1A. Out from their world of hostility they express ***their discouragement.*** *(vv. 1-11)*

    1B. Due to the apparent apathy of God *(v. 1)*

    2B. Due to the arrogant aggression of the ungodly *(vv. 2-11)*

        1C. They are prideful in their persecutions. *(vv. 2-4)*

        2C. They are presumptuous in their prosperity. *(vv. 5-7)*

        3C. They are predators after their prey. *(vv. 8-11)*

Note this continues to develop the plight of the helpless in verses 2-4, but with graphic word pictures.

            1D. Their attacks are depicted. *(vv. 8-10)*

            2D. Their atheism is deplored. *(v. 11)*

Note this is the atheistic viewpoint, compare and contrast that of the theist in verse 1.

2A. Out from their world of hope they express ***their encouragement.*** *(vv. 12-18)*

    1B. The dawning of hope for the helpless: *(vv. 12-14)*

        1C. through continuing in assertive prayers *(v. 12)*

        2C. through contemplating antithetical perspectives: *(vv. 13-14)*

            1D. those of the infidels *(v. 13)*

            2D. those of the faithful *(v. 14)*

    2B. The development of hope for the helpless: *(vv. 15-18)*

        1C. through recognizing the control of God *(vv. 15-16)*

            1D. the desire for its immediate application *(v. 15)*

            2D. the design for its ultimate application *(v. 16)*

        2C. through resting in the care of God *(vv. 17-18)*

Psalm 11

'Facing Fright with Faith not Flight'

Although two different 'voices' were speaking to David in a context of personal and national crisis, he had made up his mind to trust only in the LORD.

Introductory Affirmation: His Confidence amid Crisis *(v. 1a)*

1A. The *voices urging flight (vv. 1b-3)*
    1B. Their source *(v. 1b)*
    2B. Their substance *(vv. 1c-3)*
        1C. A command of flight *(v. 1c)*
        2C. Reasonings based on fright: *(vv. 2-3)*
            1D. a practical reason *(v. 2)*
            2D. a philosophical reason *(v. 3)*
2A. The *voice urging faith (vv. 4-7)*
    1B. A faith grounded upon the sovereignty of God *(v. 4a)*
    2B. A faith grounded upon the justice of God *(v. 4b-7)*
        1C. The principles of Divine justice *(vv. 4b-5)*
            1D. Generally applied *(v. 4b)*
            2D. Specifically applied: *(v. 5)*
                1E. to the redeemed *(v. 5a)*
                2E. to the reprobate *(v. 5b-c)*
        2C. The practice of Divine justice *(v. 6)*
        3C. The precedents of Divine justice *(v. 7a)*
        4C. The promise of Divine justice *(v. 7b)*

Psalm 12

'Man's Mouth and Our Master's Messages'

David, in Psalm 12, provides a model for passing a spiritual hearing test in that genuine disciples listen to and must properly respond to two radically different sources of speech.

1A. We can survive *the propaganda of depraved speech. (vv. 1-4)*

    1B. By prayer *(vv. 1-2)*

        1C. Its dependence *(v. 1a)*

        2C. Its documentation: *(vv. 1b-2)*

            1D. presented from the perspective of 'the victims of verbal abuse' *(v. 1b, c)*

            2D. presented from the perspective of 'the victimizers of verbal abuse' *(v. 2)*

    2B. By petition *(vv. 3-4)*

        1C. Its imprecation *(v. 3)*

        2C. Its indictments *(v. 4)*

2A. We can have security in *the protection of Divine speech. (vv. 5-8)*

    1B. Its Divine promises *(v. 5)*

        1C. Precipitated by prayer *(v. 5a)*

        2C. Presented with power *(v. 5b)*

    2B. Its Divine purity *(v. 6)*

    3B. Its Divine perseverance; balancing: *(vv. 7-8)*

        1C. our assured resources *(v. 7)*

        2C. and attendant realities *(v. 8)*

Psalm 13

'From Turmoil to Tranquility'

In Psalm 13 David is transported from the pit of peril to the promise of praise through three elevations of attitude.

1A. *David's attitude begins below 'sea level'* through the expressions of his despair. *(vv. 1-2)*

 1B. His despair is expressed through his unanswered questions about God's apparent neglect. *(v. 1)*

  1C. He senses a lack of personal concern. *(v. 1a)*

  2C. He senses a lack of personal care. *(v. 1b)*

 2B. His despair is expressed through his unanswered question about his own apparent inadequacy. *(v. 2a, b)*

 3B. His despair is expressed through his unanswered question about his opponents' apparent supremacy. *(v. 2c)*

2A. *David's attitude lifts to 'sea level'* through the expressions of his desires. *(vv. 3-4)*

 1B. His desires are voiced through petitions. *(v. 3a, b, c)*

  1C. Concentrate on me! *(v. 3a)*

  2C. Respond to me! *(v. 3b)*

  3C. Illumine me! *(v. 3c)*

 2B. His desires are vindicated through potentialities. *(vv. 3d-4)*

  1C. Concerning himself: he might die *(v. 3d)*

  2C. Concerning his opponents *(v. 4)*

   1D. They would gloat. *(v. 4a)*

   2D. They would glory. *(v. 4b)*

3A. *David's attitude climbs to 'mountain-top' level* through the expressions of his delight. *(vv. 5-6)*

 1B. His delight is displayed through attestations of faith. *(vv. 5-6a)*

  1C. His comfort in God's grace *(v. 5a)*

  2C. His confidence in God's deliverance *(v. 5b)*

  3C. His commitment to God's praise *(v. 6a)*

 2B. His delight is documented through an affirmation of fact. *(v. 6b)*

Psalm 14

'Deliberations on Depravity'

David's representative desire for deliverance *(v.7)* **in Psalm 14 constitutes the chorus to his two preceding dirges on depravity.**

1A. The *dirges on depravity (vv. 1-6)*

    1B. The first dirge comes in the form of a round and addresses the universality of depravity. *(vv. 1-3)*

        1C. The beginning of this round of dirge rises upward from earth. *(v. 1)*

            1D. Mankind's atheistic attitude *(v. 1a)*

            2D. Mankind's atheistic actions: *(v. 1b, c)*

                1E. summarized corporately *(v. 1b)*

                2E. summarized individually *(v. 1c)*

        2C. The continuing of this round of dirge resounds downward from Heaven. *(vv. 2-3)*

            1D. Heaven's investigation *(v. 2)*

                1E. The infallible Agent *(v. 2a)*

                2E. The intentional assessments *(v. 2b)*

                    1F. Testing mankind's mental morality

                    2F. Testing mankind's motivational morality

            2D. Heaven's indictments: *(v. 3)*

                1E. mankind's failure: pronounced corporately *(v. 3a)*

                2E. mankind's failure: pronounced individually *(v. 3b)*

    2B. The second dirge comes in the form of a ballad and addresses the futility of depravity. *(vv. 4-6)*

        1C. The beginning of this ballad interrogates the wicked, setting them up for judgment. *(v. 4)*

            1D. The rhetorical question to the wicked *(v. 4a; Hebrew text)*

            2D. The relational designations of the wicked: *(v. 4b, c, d; Hebrew text)*

                1E. ethically, they are adrift *(v. 4b)*

                2E. socially, they are aggressors *(v. 4c)*

                3E. theologically, they are autonomous *(v. 4d)*

2C. The continuing of this ballad implicates the wicked, separating
them out for judgment. *(vv. 5-6)*

    1D. They experience great fear. *(v. 5)*

        1E. Its inescapable reality *(v. 5a)*

        2E. Its incontestable reason *(v. 5b)*

    2D. They experience great frustration. *(v. 6)*

        1E. Their mission immediately attempted *(v. 6a)*

        2E. Their mission ultimately aborted *(v. 6b)*

2A. The *chorus on deliverance (v. 7)*

  1B. The wish for it *(v. 7a)*

  2B. The worship attending it *(v. 7b, c)*

    1C. Its timing *(v. 7b)*

    2C. Its testimonies *(v. 7c)*

Psalm 15

'The Ultimate Q & A'

Psalm 15, with its focus on moral responsibility, offers a sequence of three numbers to the combination lock of acceptable Divine worship.

1A. The combination begins with a ***two-part question***. *(v. 1)*
2A. Then turn to the 'right' with a ***twelve-part response***. *(vv. 2-5b)*

Note that this comes in two subsets of numbers.

    1B. The first ethical subset of threes *(vv. 2-3)*
        1C. Three positively phrased ethical characteristics. *(v. 2)*
            1D. His lifestyle exhibits integrity. *(v. 2a)*
            2D. His deeds exhibit justice. *(v. 2b)*
            3D. His speech exhibits reliability. *(v. 2c)*
        2C. Three negatively cast ethical characteristics. *(v. 3)*
            1D. He does not tread over people with his tongue. *(v. 3a)*
            2D. He does not harm his fellow man. *(v. 3b)*
            3D. He does not dump reproach upon someone 'near.' *(v. 3c)*
    2B. The second ethical subset of threes *(vv. 4-5b)*
        1C. Three positively phrased ethical characteristics. *(v. 4a, b, c)*
            1D. He views the reprobate as rejected. *(v. 4a)*
            2D. He respects the people of God. *(v. 4b)*
            3D. He holds himself accountable. *(v. 4c)*
        2C. Three negatively cast ethical characteristics. *(vv. 4d-5b)*
            1D. He is not fickle. *(v. 4d)*
            2D. He is not a loan shark. *(v. 5a)*
            3D. He cannot be bought. *(v. 5b)*
3A. Finally, turn back to a ***one-part guarantee***. *(v. 5c)*

Psalm 16

'Testimonies of Trust'

David's opening prayer *(v.1)* in Psalm 16 is bolstered by two cycles of testimony.

His Introductory Prayer *(v. 1)*
    Its focus *(v. 1a)*
    Its foundation *(v. 1b)*

1A. His *testimony of communion (vv. 2-4)*
    1B. Its Divine dimension *(v. 2)*
        1C. The direction of it *(v. 2a)*
        2C. The disclosures of it *(v. 2b, c)*
    2B. Its human dimension *(vv. 3-4)*
        1C. The direction of it *(v. 3)*
        2C. The disclosures of it *(v. 4)*
2A. His *testimony of confidence (vv. 5-11)*
    1B. Its past and present dimensions *(vv. 5-8)*
        1C. Concerning resources *(vv. 5-6)*
            1D. Relating to the Person of God *(v. 5)*
            2D. Relating to the providence of God *(v. 6)*
        2C. Concerning responses *(vv. 7-8)*
            1D. Relating to praise for prudence *(v. 7)*
            2D. Relating to positioning for presence *(v. 8)*
    2B. Its present and future dimensions *(vv. 9-11)*
        1C. Concerning response: joy for assurance *(v. 9)*
        2C. Concerning resources *(vv. 10-11)*
            1D. Relating to Divine intervention and death *(v. 10)*
            2D. Relating to Divine illumination and life *(v. 11)*

Psalm 17

David, seeking justice in Psalm 17, approaches the Divine Bar with three clusters of appeals.

1A. He commences his case with a cluster of appeals dealing with *response and recognition. (vv. 1-5)*
    1B. His concern for Divine responses: *(vv. 1-2)*
        1C. presented more directly *(v. 1)*
        2C. presented more indirectly *(v. 2)*
    2B. His corroborations from Divine recognitions: *(vv. 3-5)*
        1C. His motives have held up to examination. *(v. 3a, b, c)*
        2C. His mouth has held up to examination. *(v. 3d)*
        3C. His morals have held up to examination. *(vv. 4-5)*
            1D. He has avoided the wrong road. *(v. 4)*
            2D. He has adhered to the right road. *(v. 5)*
2A. He continues his case with a cluster of appeals dealing with *rescue and relief. (vv. 6-12)*
    1B. His need for rescue is presented. *(vv. 6-8)*
        1C. Expressed through his solicitations of God's attention *(v. 6)*
        2C. Expressed through his desires for God's grace *(v. 7)*
        3C. Expressed through his longings for God's care *(v. 8)*
    2B. His need for relief is documented: *(vv. 9-12)*
        1C. by the presence of his enemies *(v. 9)*
        2C. by the insensitivity of his enemies *(v. 10a)*
        3C. by the arrogance of his enemies *(v. 10b)*
        4C. by the tactics of his enemies *(v. 11)*
        5C. by the illustrations of his enemies *(v. 12)*
3A. He concludes his case with a cluster of appeals dealing with *retribution and rest. (vv. 13-15)*
    1B. His anticipation of their retribution *(vv. 13-14)*
    2B. His assurance of his rest *(v. 15)*

Psalm 18

'God is My Co-Pilot'

Between David's lift off (verses 1-3) and landing (verses 46-50) of praises to God in Psalm 18, the general trajectory of his life with the LORD ascends and descends in at least three stages.

His lift off of praises *(vv. 1-3)*

1A. Throughout the first stage *he recalls his LORD lifting him*
    out of the dark and dense atmosphere of the pit of peril. *(vv. 4-19)*
    1B. His desperation *(vv. 4-6)*
    2B. His Defender (an awesome theophanic picture of the LORD*) (vv. 7-15)*
    3B. His deliverance *(vv. 16-19)*
2A. Throughout the second stage *he revels in his LORD piloting him*
    on a lofty course through the atmosphere of ethical integrity. *(vv. 20-28)*

        Note: In their logical development, these verses unfold chiastically.

    1B. The principles of the LORD's piloting *(vv. 20-26)*
        1C. Viewed particularly from David's vantage point *(vv. 20-24)*
        2C. Viewed generally from the community's vantage point *(vv. 25-26)*
    2B. The privileges of the LORD's piloting *(vv. 27-28)*
        1C. Viewed generally from the community's vantage point *(v. 27)*
        2C. Viewed particularly from David's vantage point *(v. 28)*
3A. Throughout the third stage *he rejoices in his LORD enabling him* to
    maneuver through the turbulent atmosphere of leadership. *(vv. 29-45)*
    1B. Concerning military leadership, he rejoices in: *(vv. 29-42)*
        1C. the Power behind his power *(vv. 29-36)*
        2C. the Victor behind his victory *(vv. 37-42)*
    2B. Concerning theocratic leadership, he rejoices in: *(vv. 43-45)*
        1C. the Authority behind his authority *(v. 43)*
        2C. the Governance beyond his government *(vv. 44-45)*

His landing of praises *(vv. 46-50)*

Psalm 19

'God's Non-verbal and Verbal Communications'
Part I

Psalm 19 eloquently summarizes two prominent vehicles of God's Self-disclosure.

1A. His *general Self-disclosure* in the world *(vv. 1-6)*

    1B. The publication of the skies *(vv. 1-4b)*

        1C. Its indications *(v. 1)*

        2C. Its incessancy *(v. 2)*

        3C. Its irony *(v. 3)*

        4C. Its immensity *(vv. 4a, b)*

    2B. The prominence of the sun *(vv. 4c-6)*

        1C. Its residence *(v. 4c)*

        2C. Its resemblance *(v. 5)*

        3C. Its range *(vv. 6a, b)*

        4C. Its rays *(v. 6c)*

2A. His *special Self-disclosure* in the Word (Part II) *(vv. 7-14)*

Psalm 19

'The Word of God and the child of God'
Part II

Remember that Psalm 19 eloquently summarizes two prominent vehicles of God's Self-disclosure.

His general Self-disclosure in the world *(vv. 1-6)*
His special Self-disclosure in the Word *(vv. 7-14)*

In this second part of Psalm 19, David voices his personal gratitude to God for His Word in three ways.

1A. Objectively, he begins by *concentrating on the attributes of the Word.* *(vv. 7-8)*

> *Note the parallelism of these four lines,*
> *each expressing first what Scripture is and then what it does.*

    1B. Its instruction produces repentance *(v. 7a)*
    2B. Its witness instills wisdom *(v. 7b)*
    3B. Its oversight brings satisfaction *(v. 8a)*
    4B. Its regulation generates illumination *(v. 8b)*

2A. Subjectively, he continues by *concentrating on an appreciation of the Word.* *(vv. 9-11)*

    1B. This appreciation is based on the nature of the Word. *(vv. 9-10)*
        1C. Perceived as 'fear,' its purity is perpetual. *(v. 9a)*
        2C. Perceived as legislation *(v. 9b)*, its standards are: *(v. 9c)*
            1D. exceedingly precious *(v. 10a)*
            2D. highly palatable *(v. 10b)*
    2B. This appreciation is based on the nurture of the Word. *(v. 11)*
        1C. It is a vehicle of admonishment. *(v. 11a)*
        2C. It is a vehicle of adherence. *(v. 11b)*

3A. Implicationally, he concludes by *concentrating on the application of the Word.* *(vv. 12-14)*

    1B. Being 'in the Word' exposes the sin of the child of God, pushing him to prayer. *(vv. 12-13)*
    2B. Being 'in the Word' confirms the salvation of the child of God, propelling him to praise. *(v. 14)*

Psalm 20

'The Battle Before'

Psalm 20, in anticipation of a military campaign, commemorates a three-phased ceremony of Israel conducted in the presence of the Commander-in-Chief on behalf of their king-general.

1A. This ceremony *commenced with an offering of their prayers. (vv. 1-5)*
    1B. Prayer for the king's protection *(vv. 1-2)*
    2B. Prayer for the king's presents *(v. 3)*
    3B. Prayer for the king's plans *(v. 4)*
    4B. Prayer for the king's prosperity *(v. 5)*
        1C. Its expectations *(v. 5a, b)*
        2C. Its expression *(v. 5c)*
2A. This ceremony *continued with a confirmation of their confidence. (vv. 6-8)*
    1B. Solo expressions of it *(v. 6)*
    2B. Corporate expressions of it *(vv. 7-8)*
        1C. Conveyed through outlook *(v. 7)*
        2C. Conveyed through outcome *(v. 8)*
3A. This ceremony *concluded with a reaffirmation of their dependence. (v. 9)*

Psalm 21

'The Battle Behind (and Before Again)'

In Psalm 21, two scenarios of victory provide a context for praise and prayer to the Commander-in-Chief of Israel's king-general.

1A. *A present-past scenario of praise* is grounded upon victories accomplished in the LORD. *(vv. 1-6)*

    1B. The celebration of these accomplished victories in the LORD *(v. 1)*

    2B. The commemoration of these accomplished victories in the LORD *(vv. 2-6)*

        1C. A commemoration of answers to prayer *(vv. 2-4)*

        2C. A commemoration of attestations of providence *(vv. 5-6)*

2A. *A present-future scenario of prayer* and praise is grounded upon victories anticipated in the LORD *(vv. 7-13)*

    1B. The king's confidence and anticipated victories in the LORD *(v. 7)*

    2B. The Commander-in-Chief's cause and anticipated victories in the LORD *(vv. 8-12)*

        1C. Enemies will be exposed according to His cause. *(v. 8)*

        2C. Enemies will be judged according to His cause. *(vv. 9-10)*

        3C. Enemies will be frustrated according to His cause. *(v. 11)*

        4C. Enemies will be repelled according to His cause. *(v. 12)*

    3B. The people's concord and anticipated victories in the LORD *(v. 13)*

Psalm 22

'God-forsaken'
Part I

By three merging mixtures the psalmist's mood shifts from the pits through prayer to praise.

1A. As *he mixes his hopelessness with history*, an ember of encouragement is spared paving the way for prayer. *(vv. 1-10)*

    1B. His hopelessness and national history *(vv. 1-5)*

        1C. Present experience *(vv. 1-2)*

        2C. Past encouragements *(vv. 3-5)*

    2B. His hopelessness and natal history *(vv. 6-10)*

        1C. Present experiences *(vv. 6-8)*

        2C. Past encouragements *(vv. 9-10)*

2A. As *he mixes his prayers with persecutions*, God responds paving the way for praise. *(vv. 11-21)*

    1B. His first prayer weakly originates from a no-help outlook. *(vv. 11-18)*

        1C. Its brevity *(v. 11a)*

        2C. Its burden *(vv. 11b-18)*

            1D. Summarized *(vv. 11b, c)*

            2D. Illustrated: *(vv. 12-18)*

                1E. his first wave of illustration *(vv. 12-18)*

                    1F. The reality of bestial attackers *(vv. 12-13)*

                    2F. The results of bestial attacks *(vv. 14-15)*

                2E. his second wave of illustration *(vv. 16-18)*

                    1F. The reality of bestial attackers *(vv. 16-18)*

                    2F. The results of bestial attacks *(v. 17)*

    2B. His second prayer wonderfully originates from a Divine help outlook. *(vv. 19-21)*

3A. As *he mixes praise with answered prayer*, testimonies arise paving the way for a legacy of true worship. *(vv. 22-31)*

Psalm 22

'God-found and filled'
Part II

By three merging mixtures the psalmist's mood shifts from the pits through prayer to praise.

1A. As *he mixes his hopelessness with history*, an ember of encouragement is sparked paving the way for prayer. *(vv. 1-10)*

2A. As *he mixes his prayers with persecutions*, God responds paving the way for praise. *(vv. 11-21)*

  1B. His first prayer weakly originates from a no-help outlook. *(vv. 11-18)*

  2B. His second prayer wonderfully originates from a Divine help outlook. *(vv. 19-21)*

  1C. Its repetitions *(vv. 19-21a)*

  2C. Its results *(v. 21b)*

3A. As *he mixes praise with answered prayer*, testimonies arise paving the way for a legacy of true worship. *(vv. 22-31)*

  1B. An individual precipitation of praise *(vv. 22-25)*

  1C. Its personal commitment *(v. 22)*

  2C. Its personal challenge: *(vv. 23-24)*

  1D. through delivery *(v. 23)*

  2D. through documentation *(v. 24)*

  3C. Its personal celebration *(v. 25)*

  2B. A corporate perpetuation of praise *(vv. 26-31)*

  1C. Its testimony expands geographically resulting in true worship. *(vv. 26-28)*

  1D. The growth of such testimony *(vv. 26-27)*

  1E. Throughout the community *(v. 26)*

  2E. Throughout the cosmos *(v. 27)*

  2D. The Grounds of such testimony *(v. 28)*

  2C. Its testimony expands genealogically resulting in true worship. *(vv. 29-31)*

  1D. The concluding praises of a current generation *(v. 29)*

  2D. The commencing praises from coming generations *(vv. 30-31)*

Psalm 23

'The Unique Shepherd-KING-Host'

Using some common ancient near-eastern images in Psalm 23, David progressively unveils his personal relationship with the LORD in three stages.

1A. In the first stage *he introduces <u>both</u> the theology of and his trust* in the unique Shepherd-KING-Host. *(v. 1)*

    1B. He condenses his theology of the LORD
    (cf. an expansion of his theology in verses 2-3).

    2B. He capsulizes his trust in the LORD
    (cf. an expansion of his trust in verses 4-6).

2A. In the second stage *he illuminates his theology* of the unique Shepherd-KING-Host. *(v. 2-3b)*

    1B. He illumines it metaphorically. *(v. 2)*

        1C. God's grace *(v. 2a)*

        2C. God's guidance *(v. 2b)*

    2B. He illumines it metaphysically. *(v. 3)*

        1C. God's grace *(v. 3a)*

        2C. God's guidance *(v. 3b)*

3A. In the third stage *he illustrates his trust* in the unique Shepherd-KING-Host. *(vv. 4-6)*

    1B. Personal peril is overcome by PERSONAL Presence and protection. *(v. 4)*

    2B. Personal pressure is overshadowed by PERSONAL provision. *(v. 5)*

    3B. Personal privilege is obviated by PERSONAL pursuit. *(v. 6)*

Psalm 24

Psalm 24 traces the community's worship procession, both spatially and spiritually, through three progressive stages.

1A. During stage one *they worship the Creator through contemplation.* *(vv. 1-2)*

    1B. They contemplate His ownership of everything. *(v. 1)*

        1C. They recognize the scope of His ownership. *(v. 1a)*

        2C. They respect the sovereignty of His ownership. *(v. 1b)*

    2B. They contemplate His origination of everything. *(v. 2)*

        1C. He provided mankind's terrain. *(v. 2a)*

        2C. He prepared mankind's terrain. *(v. 2b)*

2A. During stage two *they worship the Savior through consecration.* *(vv. 3-6)*

    1B. The probing questions inviting consecration *(v. 3)*

        1C. Who can approach Him? *(v. 3a)*

        2C. Who can abide with Him? *(v. 3b)*

    2B. The proper qualities indicating consecration: *(vv. 4-6)*

        1C. with a focus upon individual consecration *(vv. 4-5)*

            1D. He is described by behavior. *(v. 4)*

            2D. He is disclosed by blessing. *(v. 5)*

        2C. with a focus upon corporate consecration *(v. 6)*

3A. During stage three *they worship the King through commemoration.* *(vv. 7-10)*

    1B. The first chorus commemorating the King *(vv. 7-8)*

        1C. The King is welcomed via bold personification. *(v. 7)*

        2C. The King is worshipped because of His performance. *(v. 8)*

            1D. The question about His performance *(v. 8a)*

            2D. The response about His performance *(v. 8b)*

    2B. The second chorus commemorating the King *(vv. 9-10)*

        1C. The King is welcomed via bold personification. *(v. 9)*

        2C. The King is worshipped because of His primacy. *(v. 10)*

            1D. The question about His primacy *(v. 10a)*

            2D. The response about His primacy *(v. 10b)*

Psalm 25

'Trust Triumphs over Troubles'

In Psalm 25, let's journey with David through three familiar landscapes of life's challenging highways and byways so that we also might learn that trust triumphs over troubles.

1A. In verses 1-7 we *join David in the gully of trial.*
    1B. The realities of the gully of trial *(vv. 1-3)*
    2B. The road map out of the gully of trial *(vv. 4-7)*
        1C. The LORD's guidance *(vv. 4-5)*
        2C. The LORD's grace *(vv. 6-7)*
2A. In verses 8-15 we *travel with David on the mountain of confidence. (vv. 8-15)*
    1B. As David ascends this mountain he has confidence in the Person of God. *(vv. 8-11)*
        1C. David's adoration *(vv. 8-10)*
        2C. David's application *(v. 11)*
    2B. As David descends this mountain he has confidence in the provisions of God. *(vv. 12-15)*
        1C. David's affiliation *(i.e. this confidence in God's provisions is viewed from the corporate perspective) (vv. 12-14)*
        2C. David's application *(i.e. this confidence in God's provisions is viewed from the individual perspective) (v. 15)*
3A. In verses 16-22 we *continue with David through the valley of trouble. (vv. 16-22)*
    1B. The horrible terrain of the valley of trouble *(vv. 16b, 17a, 18b, 19b)*
    2B. The hopeful transportation through the valley of trouble *(vv. 16a, 17b, 18a, 19a, 20-22)*

Scroggie: 'Always place God between you and your troubles and enemies.'

Psalm 26

In Psalm 26, four volleys of intermingling prayers and proofs reveal the psalmist's passion to worship the LORD in spirit and in truth.

1A. An *introductory volley reveals his situation.* *(v. 1)*
    1B. His prayer for justice *(v. 1a)*
    2B. His proofs of commitment *(v. 1b)*
2A. A more *detailed volley reveals his transparency.* *(vv. 2-8)*
    1B. His prayers for scrutiny *(v. 2)*
    2B. His proofs of loyalty *(vv. 3-8)*
        1C. His dependence upon God *(v. 3)*
        2C. His discernment among men *(vv. 4-5)*
        3C. His desire for communion: *(vv. 6-8)*
            1D. its methods anticipated *(vv. 6-7)*
            2D. its motive affirmed *(v. 8)*
3A. His *eschatological volley reveals his outlook.* *(vv. 9-11a)*
    1B. His prayers for final favor *(v. 9)*
    2B. His proofs of measurable difference *(vv. 10-11a)*
        1C. Their characteristic conduct *(v. 10)*
        2C. His continued commitment *(v. 11a)*
4A. His *concluding volley reveals his confidence.* *(vv. 11b–12)*
    1B. His prayers show confidence in the Person of God. *(v. 11b)*
    2B. His proofs show confidence in the provision of God. *(v. 12)*
        1C. His divinely enabled walk *(v. 12a)*
        2C. His divinely enabled worship *(v. 12b)*

Psalm 27

Part I

In Psalm 27, the psalmist, in the presence of his LORD, engages in three conversations which help him balance the ups and downs of real life.

1A. He converses with himself about *privileges. (vv. 1-6)*
    1B. The privilege of Divine confidence *(vv. 1-3)*
        1C. Its basis *(v. 1)*
            1D. The LORD's provisions *(v. 1a)*
            2D. The LORD's protection *(v. 1b)*
        2C. Its history *(vv. 2-3)*
            1D. A past actualization *(v. 2)*
            2D. A future anticipation *(v. 3)*
    2B. The privilege of Divine communion *(vv. 4-6)*
        1C. The resolve *(v. 4)*
        2C. The response *(v. 5)*
        3C. The results *(v. 6)*
            1D. Protection *(v. 6a)*
            2D. Praise *(v. 6b)*
2A. He converses with the LORD about *problems. (vv. 7-12)*
3A. He converses with himself about *perseverance. (vv. 13-14)*

Psalm 27

Part II

In Psalm 27, the psalmist, in the presence of his LORD, engages in three conversations which help him balance the ups and downs of real life.

1A. He converses with himself about *privileges*. *(vv. 1-6)*

2A. He converses with the LORD about *problems*. *(vv. 7-12)*

    1B. Through general prayers *(vv. 7-10)*

        1C. His positively phrased prayers *(vv. 7-8)*

            1D. Their brevity *(v. 7)*

            2D. Their basis *(v. 8)*

        2C. His negatively phrased prayers *(vv. 9-10)*

            1D. Their concerns *(v. 9)*

            2D. Their confidence *(v. 10)*

    2B. Through particular prayers *(vv. 11-12)*

        1C. His positively phrased prayers *(v. 11)*

            1D. Their needs *(v. 11a)*

            2D. Their necessity *(v. 11b)*

        2C. His negatively phrased prayer *(v. 12)*

            1D. Its need *(v. 12a)*

            2D. Its necessity *(v. 12b)*

3A. He converses with himself about *perseverance*. *(vv. 13-14)*

    1B. The past precedent of his perseverance *(v. 13)*

    2B. The future promise of his perseverance *(v. 14)*

Psalm 28

Moving through two cycles of crisis and confidence the Psalmist magnifies the justice of God.

1A. The first cycle is *individual in outlook* and terminates in praise. *(vv. 1-7)*
    1B. His personal crisis *(vv. 1-5b)*
        1C. His requests for attention *(vv. 1-2)*
        2C. His requests for discrimination *(vv. 3-5b)*
            1D. Their immediate concerns *(vv 3-4)*
                1E. Conveyed through protestations of innocence *(v. 3)*
                2E. Conveyed through prayers of imprecation *(v. 4)*
            2D. Their ultimate grounds *(v. 5a, b)*
    2B. His personal confidence *(vv. 5c-7)*
        1C. Concerning ultimate justice *(v. 5c)*
        2C. Concerning immediate praise *(vv. 6-7)*
2A. The second cycle is *corporate in outlook* and terminates in prayer. *(vv. 8-9)*
    1B. His reassurance in the light of corporate confidence *(v. 8)*
    2B. His requests in the face of corporate crisis *(v. 9)*

Psalm 29

Three representative realms of the supremacy of God in Psalm 29 develop the propriety of praise to YAHWEH alone.

1A. The LORD's *supremacy over heavenly beings* commands praise. *(vv. 1-2)*

2A. The LORD's *supremacy over the 'forces of nature'* consummates in praise. *(vv. 3-9)*

  1B. The manifestations of His supremacy over the 'forces of nature' are exhibited. *(vv. 3-9b)*

  1C. Looking to the West, He reigns supreme over the sea. *(v. 3)*

  2C. Looking to the North, He reigns supreme over the high country. *(vv. 4-7)*

  3C. Looking to the South, He reigns supreme over the desert country. *(vv. 8-9b)*

  2B. The magnification of His supremacy over the 'forces of nature' is expressed. *(v. 9c)*

3A. The LORD's *supremacy over humanity* calls for praise. *(vv. 10-11)*

  1B. Because of His position *(v. 10)*

  1C. He was enthroned over the great flood. *(v. 10a)*

  2C. He remains enthroned over all history. *(v. 10b)*

  2B. Because of His provisions: *(v. 11)*

  1C. protection *(v. 11a)*

  2C. peace *(v. 11b)*

Psalm 30

The psalmist's beginning and ending pledges to praise, bookend two directional vantage points on his prayers and testimonies.

Note his launching praise (v. 1a) and his landing praise (v. 12b)

His launching praise *(v.1a)*

1A. His opening pledge to praise looks back upon *historic prayers and testimonies.* *(vv. 1b-9)*
    1B. His individual remembrance *(vv. 1b-3)*
        1C. His past prayer *(v. 2a)*
        2C. His past answers *(vv. 1b, 2b-3)*
    2B. His public reminders:
        1C. their responsibilities *(v. 4)*
        2C. their reasonings *(v. 5)*
    3B. His individual reflections *(vv. 6-9)*
        1C. Recognized pride *(v. 6)*
        2C. Regained perspective *(v. 7)*
        3C. Return to prayer *(vv. 8-9)*
            1D. His resolves *(v. 8)*
            2D. His reasonings *(v. 9)*
2A. His concluding pledge to praise looks ahead to *continuing prayers and testimonies.* *(vv. 10-12a)*
    1B. His petitions *(v. 10)*
    2B. His precedent *(v. 11)*
    3B. His purpose *(v. 12a)*
        1C. Positively stated
        2C. Negatively stated

His landing praise *(v. 12b)*

Psalm 31

Within the two settings of Psalm 31, the Psalmist's testimonies passionately celebrate the sufficiencies of God.

1A. The originally *private setting* behind these testimonies *(vv. 1-18)*
    1B. His testimony about security and salvation *(vv. 1-5)*
        1C. His history of dependence *(v. 1a)*
        2C. His habit of dependence: prayer *(vv. 1b-2)*
        3C. His hope and dependence *(vv. 3-5)*
    2B. His testimony about discernment and deliverance *(vv. 6-8)*
        1C. Its statement *(vv. 6-7a)*
        2C. Its support *(vv. 7b-8)*
    3B. His testimony about reproach and relief *(vv. 9-18)*
        1C. His testimony from a horizontal perspective *(vv. 9-13)*
            1D. It begins briefly with a request for mercy. *(v. 9a)*
            2D. It continues extensively with reasons for mercy. *(vv. 9b-13)*
        2C. His testimony from a vertical and horizontal perspective *(vv. 14-18)*
            1D. It begins initially with affirmations of faith. *(v. 14-15a)*
            2D. It continues concurrently with appeals for justice. *(vv. 15b-18)*
2A. The ultimately *public setting* for these testimonies *(vv. 19-14)*
    1B. His testimonies and Divine exaltation *(vv. 19-22)*
        1C. General affirmation *(vv. 19-20)*
        2C. Special application *(vv. 21-22)*
    2B. His testimonies and exhortation *(vv. 23-24)*

Psalm 32

Life's most important lessons about sin, confession, and forgiveness are skillfully shared by David through two avenues of approach in Psalm 32.

1A. Through David's first avenue of approach these *lessons are remembered*. *(vv. 1-5)*

Note that if these remembrances would have been presented in a chronological or historical order of experience the sequence would be verses 3-4; verse 5; then verses 1-2.

    1B. Personal lessons about results are remembered. *(vv. 1-2)*
    2B. Personal lessons about resistance are remembered. *(vv. 3-4)*
    3B. Personal lessons about responses are remembered. *(v. 5)*

Note the chiastic (i.e. inverted) order of responses, resistance, and finally, results in the second part of this Psalm.

2A. Through David's second avenue of approach these *lessons are relayed*. *(vv. 6-11)*
    1B. General lessons about responses are relayed. *(vv. 6-7)*
        1C. Responding with prayer *(v. 6)*
        2C. Responding to protection *(v. 7)*
    2B. General lessons about resistance are relayed. *(vv. 8-9)*
        1C. The instructor *(v. 8)*
        2C. The instruction *(v. 9)*
    3B. General lessons about results are relayed. *(vv. 10-11)*
        1C. The results are contrasted. *(v. 10)*
        2C. The results are celebrated. *(v. 11)*

Psalm 33

In Psalm 33, its praise prelude and prayer finale provide the surround-sound of worship for three choruses of rationale.

A praise prelude *(vv. 1-3)*

1A. A general chorus briefly introduces *the themes of rationale. (vv. 4-5)*
    1B. The theme of His sovereign power in 'natural' history *(v. 4)*
    (cf. its expanding chorus in verses 6-9)
    2B. The theme of His sovereign providence over human history *(v. 5)*
    (cf. its expanding chorus in verses 10-19)
2A. A special chorus sings *the theme of the Creator's sovereign power. (vv. 6-9)*
    1B. The grand choir surveys His sovereign power. *(vv. 6-7)*
    2B. The antiphonal choir sings of a proper response. *(v. 8)*
    3B. The grand choir summarizes His sovereign power. *(v. 9)*
3A. A special chorus sings *the theme of the Creator's sovereign providence. (vv. 10-19)*
    1B. The grand choir surveys His sovereign providence. *(vv. 10-11)*
        1C. Man's plans sit on sand. *(v. 10)*
        2C. God's plans are set in concrete. *(v. 11)*
    2B. The antiphonal choir sings of a proper response. *(v. 12)*
    3B. The grand choir summarizes His sovereign providence. *(vv. 13-19)*
        1C. Inferred from His evaluative vantage points: *(vv. 13-15)*
            1D. from His throne above *(vv. 13-14)*
            2D. from His access within *(v. 15)*
        2C. Illustrated by His ethical precedents: *(vv. 16-19)*
            1D. applied to those living independently *(vv. 16-17)*
            2D. applied to those living dependently *(vv. 18-19)*

A prayer finale: *(vv. 20-22)*
    its spirit *(vv. 20-21)*
    its substance *(v. 22)*

Psalm 34

Through two forms of sharing, the psalmist shows that submitting to the LORD is the key to surviving real life in the real world.

1A. Through *his testimony* he shares this key. *(vv. 1-10)*

    1B. His personal testimony of praise calls for a public chorus. *(vv. 1-3)*

        1C. His solo *(vv. 1-2)*

        2C. His solicitation *(v. 3)*

    2B. His individual testimonies of answered prayer call for corporate complements. *(vv. 4-10)*

        1C. His first recollection calls for responses leading to relief. *(vv. 4-5)*

            1D. His past relief *(v. 4)*

            2D. Their potential relief *(v. 5)*

        2C. His second recollection calls for responses leading to reward. *(vv. 6-10)*

            1D. His past reward *(v. 6)*

            2D. Their potential reward *(vv. 7-10)*

                1E. Their resource *(v. 7)*

                2E. Their responsibilities *(vv. 8-10)*

2A. Through *his teaching* he shares this key. *(vv. 11-22)*

    1B. The invitation to his teaching *(v. 11)*

    2B. The interrogation leading into his teaching *(v. 12)*

    3B. The instructions of his teaching *(vv. 13-22)*

        1C. Important responsibilities *(vv. 13-14)*

        2C. Important recognitions: *(vv. 15-22)*

            1D. concerning Divine attention *(vv. 15-17)*

            2D. concerning Divine compassion and care *(vv. 18-20)*

            3D. concerning Divine justice *(vv. 21-22)*

Psalm 35

Three cycles of exasperation and expectation in Psalm 35 convey the psalmist's prayers about his persecutors to God.

1A. The first cycle comes in response to *the attacks he was experiencing. (vv. 1-10)*
    1B. He prays for defense. *(vv. 1-3)*
    2B. He prays for retribution. *(vv. 4-8)*
    3B. He pledges praise. *(vv. 9-10)*
2A. The second cycle comes in response to *the perjury he was experiencing. (vv. 11-18)*
    1B. He prays that God would examine the evidence. *(vv. 11-16)*
        1C. By examining them *(vv. 11-12)*
        2C. By examining him *(vv. 13-14)*
        3C. By re-examining them *(vv. 15-16)*
    2B. He prays that God would act without delay. *(v. 17)*
    3B. He pledges praise. *(v. 18)*
3A. The third cycle comes in response to *the mockery he was anticipating. (vv. 19-28)*
    1B. He prays for judgment concerning them. *(vv. 19-21)*
    2B. He prays for justice concerning them. *(vv. 22-26)*
    3B. He pledges praise. *(vv. 27-28)*
        1C. From the community *(v. 27)*
        2C. From himself *(v. 28)*

Psalm 36

David's two different moods in Psalm 36 exemplify his continuing quest for balance concerning the realities of human wickedness and Divine benevolence.

1A. We pick David up in *a mood of deliberation.* *(vv. 1-9)*
    1B. His deliberations on human infidelity *(vv. 1-4)*
        1C. Its 'song' *(v. 1)*
        2C. Its symptoms: *(vv. 2-4)*
            1D. corrupt character *(v. 2)*
            2D. corrupt communications *(v. 3a)*
            3D. corrupt conduct *(vv. 3b-4)*

> *Now comes the whiplash in David's deliberations as he*
> *very abruptly moves from human meanness to Divine mercy.*

    2B. His deliberations on Divine fidelity *(vv. 5-9)*
        1C. Its 'song' *(vv. 5-6b)*

> *Note the anthem of attributes.*

        2C. Its samples: *(vv. 6c-9)*
            1D. God's protection of all life *(v. 6c)*
            2D. God's provisions for human life *(vv. 7-9)*
                1E. Exclaimed *(v. 7a)*
                2E. Enjoyed *(vv. 7b-9)*
2A. We leave David in *a mood of dependence.* *(vv. 10-12)*
    1B. Implemental through prayer *(vv. 10-11)*
        1C. For the people *(v. 10)*
        2C. For himself *(v. 11)*
    2B. Intimated through perspective *(v. 12)*

Psalm 37

In Psalm 37 David mixes and matches six stylistic vehicles in order to advance its major message on the eventual arrival of Divine Justice.

1A. An *introductory overview* (*vv. 1-2*)
    1B. Responsibilities (*v. 1*)
    2B. Reasonings (*v. 2*)
2A. An *initial expansion* (*vv. 3-11*)
    1B. Responsibilities and reasonings stemming from the relationship between the LORD and the righteous (*vv. 3-6*)
    2B. Responsibilities and reasonings stemming from the relationship between the LORD, the righteous and the wicked (*vv. 7-11*)
3A. Some *proverbial perspectives* (*vv. 12-24*)
    1B. The LORD will handle the hostile.
    (*vv. 12-15*)
    2B. The LORD will differentiate between the hostile and the humble.
    (*vv. 16-22*)
    3B. The LORD will help the humble.
    (*vv. 23-24*)
4A. An *initial testimony* (*vv. 25-26*)
5A. A *final expansion* (*vv. 27-34*)
    1B. Responsibilities and reasonings stemming from the relationship between the LORD and the righteous (*vv. 27-31*)
    2B. Responsibilities and reasonings stemming from the relationship between the LORD, the righteous, and the wicked (*vv. 32-34*)
6A. A *final testimony* (*vv. 35-40*)
    1B. About the ultimate destiny of the wicked (*vv. 35-36*)
    2B. About the true state of the righteous (*v. 37*)
    3B. About the certainty of Divine intervention (*vv. 38-40*)
        1C. In a negative way concerning the wicked (*v. 38*)
        2C. In a positive way concerning the righteous (*vv. 39-40*)

Psalm 38

David's opening and closing prayers in Psalm 38 respectively relate to two onslaughts of enemies.

His introductory prayer flows into his first onslaught. *(vv. 1-2)*
    Its expressions *(v. 1)*
    Its explanations *(v. 2)*

1A. His first onslaught comes from *the enemy within.* *(vv. 3-10)*
    1B. Evidences of it *(vv. 3-8)*
        1C. His condition and its assumed causes *(vv. 3-5)*
        2C. His condition and its attendant consternation *(vv. 6-8)*
    2B. Exposure of it *(vv. 9-10)*
2A. His second onslaught comes from *enemies without.* *(vv. 11-20)*
    1B. He was betrayed by 'friends.' *(v. 11)*
    2B. He was besieged by foes. *(vv. 12-20)*
        1C. They are described comparatively. *(vv. 12-18)*
            1D. Their resolves *(v. 12)*
            2D. His responses *(vv. 13-18)*
                1E. To their pressures *(vv. 13-14)*
                2E. To God's providence *(vv. 15-18)*
        2C. They are described numerically. *(v. 19)*
        3C. They are described ethically. *(v. 20)*

His concluding prayers flow out of his second onslaught. *(vv. 21-22)*
    Negatively expressed *(v. 21)*
    Positively expressed *(v. 22)*

Psalm 39

In this lament David breaks his initial silence with two heavy-duty rounds of requests and reflections about the brevity and burdens of life.

Introduction: David's silence *(vv. 1-3)*
    His commitments to silence *(v. 1)*
    The consequences of his silence *(vv. 2-3)*
        Their frustration *(vv. 2-3b)*
        Their fruition *(v. 3c)*

1A. *Round one* of his requests and reflections about the brevity and burdens of life. *(vv. 4-6)*
    1B. His request for perspective *(v. 4)*
    2B. His reflections on perspective *(vv. 5-6)*
        1C. Personalized *(v. 5a-b)*
        2C. Generalized *(vv. 5c-6)*
2A. *Round two* of his requests and reflections about the brevity and burdens of life. *(vv. 7-13)*
    1B. His reflection on hope *(v. 7)*
    2B. His requests and reflections on providence *(vv. 8-11)*
        1C. Personalized *(vv. 8-10)*
        2C. Generalized *(vv. 11)*
    3B. His requests for relief *(vv. 12-13)*
        1C. Positively couched *(v. 12)*
        2C. Negatively couched *(v. 13)*

Psalm 40

Two situations constitute the framework for the psalmist's publicized expressions of worship in Psalm 40.

1A. He first appeals to *a precedent from a past situation. (vv. 1-10)*

    1B. The merciful rescue by God *(vv. 1-3)*

        1C. The experience of the 'one' *(vv. 1-3a)*

        2C. The expectation for the 'many' *(v. 3b)*

    2B. The multiple resources in God *(vv. 4-5)*

        1C. Viewed from the perspective of the 'one' *(v. 4)*

        2C. Viewed from the perspective of the 'many' *(v. 5)*

    3B. The motivational responses to God *(vv. 6-10)*

        1C. Directly, of the 'one' to God *(vv. 6-8)*

        2C. Indirectly, of the one through the 'many' *(vv. 9-10)*

2A. He then applies it to *his prayers for a present situation. (vv. 11-17)*

    1B. His prayers and his circumstances *(vv. 11-12)*

        1C. These circumstances intensified his desires. *(v. 11)*

        2C. These circumstances indicated his desperation. *(v. 12)*

    2B. His prayers and his communities *(vv. 13-17)*

        1C. He offers prayers from the context of his hostile 'community.' *(vv. 13-15)*

        2C. He offers prayers from the context of his hopeful community. *(vv. 16-17)*

            1D. His prayers involving the 'many' *(v. 16)*

            2D. His prayers intended for the 'one' *(v. 17)*

Psalm 41

In Psalm 41, seven installments of four basic forms bear along David's message of God's TLC in the critical care unit of life.

1A. In David's first *installment of eulogy* he recognizes human compassion. *(v. 1a)*

2A. In David's first *installment of confidence* he revels in God's TLC for anyone who is compassionate. *(vv. 1b-3)*

3A. In David's first *installment of prayer* he requests grace, health, and forgiveness. *(v. 4)*

4A. In David's first and only *installment of lament* he rehearses the meanness that he has experienced in his social contexts. *(vv. 5-9)*

    1B. He rehearses his experiences with his opponents: *(vv. 5-8)*

        1C. emphasizing their desire *(v. 5)*

        2C. emphasizing their hypocrisy *(v. 6)*

        3C. emphasizing their conspiracy *(v. 7)*

        4C. emphasizing their allegation *(v. 8)*

    2B. He rehearses his experience with his close companion. *(v. 9)*

5A. In David's final *installment of prayer* he requests grace, health and retribution. *(v. 10)*

6A. In David's final *installment of confidence* he revels in God's TLC for him personally. *(vv. 11-12)*

7A. In David's final *installment of eulogy* he recognizes Divine compassion. *(v. 13)*

Psalm 42

Psalm 42 is a dirge of two verses sung to the tune of 'echoes of doubt and whispers of hope.'

1A. In verse one *the psalmist sings of his drought.* *(vv. 1-5)*
    1B. The content of this verse *(vv. 1-4)*
        1C. His need of refreshment *(vv. 1-3)*
            1D. He had no 'sweet water' *(vv. 1-2)*
            2D. He had too much 'bitter water' *(v. 3)*
        2C. His attempt through reminiscence *(v. 4)*
    2B. The chorus of this dirge *(v. 5)*
        1C. Its transparent realization *(v. 5a-b)*
        2C. Its transcendent remedy *(v. 5c-d)*
2A. In verse two *the psalmist sings of his drowning.* *(vv. 6-11)*
    1B. The content of this verse *(vv. 6-10)*
        1C. His attempt through reminiscence *(vv. 6-8)*
            1D. Its future orientation *(v. 6)*
            2D. Its current orientation *(v. 7)*
            3D. Its historic orientation *(v. 8)*
        2C. His need of remembrance *(vv. 9-10)*
            1D. Its vertical confirmation *(v. 9)*
            2D. Its horizontal corroboration *(v. 10)*
    2B. The chorus of this dirge *(v. 11)*
        1C. Its transparent realization *(v. 11 a-b; cf. v. 5 a-b)*
        2C. Its transcendent remedy *(v. 11 c-d; cf. v. 5 c-d)*

Psalm 43

By interrelating the psalmist's two modes of communication in Psalm 43 and comparing them with the laments of Psalm 42, we observe indications of progress as he continued to deal with his despondency.

1A. Listening in on his first mode *we hear his prayers to God. (vv. 1-4)*
  1B. The first round of his prayers deals with righting wrongs. *(vv. 1-2)*
    1C. His requests *(v. 1)*
    2C. His reasonings: *(v. 2)*
      1D. positively laid out *(v. 2a)*
      2D. negatively laid out: *(v. 2b-c)*
        1E. 'why rejection?!' *(v. 2b)*
        2E. 'why dejection?!' *(v. 2c)*
  2B. The second round of his prayers deals with restoring 'rights'. *(vv. 3-4)*
    1C. His requests *(v. 3)*
    2C. His reasonings *(v. 4)*
2A. Listening in on his second mode *we hear his 'pep-talk' to himself. (v. 5)*
  1B. Including exhortation *(v. 5a-b)*
  2B. Including encouragement *(v. 5c-d)*

Psalm 44

By employing three historical foci in Psalm 44, the psalmist tries to understand and deal with a national tragedy.

1A. By *focusing on past history* he only amplifies the shock of this national tragedy. *(vv. 1-8)*

    1B. The events from past history: *(vv. 1-3)*

        1C. traditionally supplied *(v. 1a-b)*

        2C. temporally surveyed *(vv. 1c-2)*

        3C. theologically summarized *(v. 3)*

    2B. The effects of past history: *(vv. 4-8)*

        1C. acknowledging them *(vv. 4-5)*

        2C. applying them *(v. 6)*

        3C. affirming them *(vv. 7-8)*

2A. By *focusing on current history* he is overwhelmed by the inscrutability of this national tragedy. *(vv. 9-22)*

    1B. What God did was painfully clear. *(vv. 9-16)*

        1C. He apparently had resigned from being their Divine Warrior. *(v. 9)*

        2C. He apparently caused them to be devastated. *(vv. 10-12)*

        3C. He apparently made them a laughingstock. *(vv. 13-16)*

    2B. Why God did it was provokingly unclear. *(vv. 17-22)*

        1C. Their responsibility was apparently rewarded with His cursings. *(vv. 17-19)*

        2C. Their remembrance was apparently rewarded with His crushings. *(vv. 20-22)*

3A. By *focusing on future history* he desperately prays for an end to this national tragedy. *(vv. 23-26)*

    1B. He boldly seeks Divine attention. *(vv. 23-25)*

        1C. His demands *(v. 23)*

        2C. His documentations: *(vv. 24-25)*

            1D. philosophically stated through questions *(v. 24)*

            2D. practically stated through realities *(v. 25)*

    2B. He boldly seeks Divine intervention. *(v. 26)*

Psalm 45

Upon the occasion of a royal wedding, the psalmist offers a three-part song of celebration.

His poetic preface *(v. 1)*

1A. In the first part *he sings about the king-groom.* *(vv. 2-9)*
    1B. This part of his song first eulogizes the endowments of the king-groom. *(v. 2)*
    2B. This part of his song also encourages the exploits of the king-groom. *(vv. 3-5)*
    3B. This part of his song further extols the elevation of the king-groom. *(vv. 6-7)*
        1C. An affirmation about his dynasty *(v. 7)*
        2C. An affirmation about his dignity *(v. 8)*
    4B. This part of his song finally exhibits the eminence of the king-groom. *(vv. 8-9)*
2A. In the second part *he sings about the princess-bride.* *(vv. 10-15)*
    1B. This part of his song relays a challenge to the princess-bride. *(vv. 10-12)*
        1C. Its responsibilities *(vv. 10-11)*
        2C. Its rewards *(v. 12)*
    2B. This part of his song recounts the procession of the princess-bride. *(vv. 13-15)*
3A. In the third part *he sings about future children* from this union. *(v. 16)*

His poetic postscript *(v. 17)*

Psalm 46

The major burden of Psalm 46 is that God provides stability for His people who live in two exceedingly unstable environments.

1A. In the unstable environment of nature *He is our Solid Rock of stability.* *(vv. 1-3)*

    1B. The affirmation of His stability *(v. 1)*

    2B. The application of His stability *(vv. 2-3)*

        1C. The testimony of our faith *(v. 2a)*

        2C. The tests of our faith *(vv. 2b-3)*

            1D. By smashing earthquakes *(v. 2b)*

            2D. By surging floods *(v. 3)*

2A. In the unstable environment of the nations *He is our Sole Resource of stability.* *(vv. 4-11)*

    1B. The first chorus of confidence about God being our Sole Resource of stability *(vv. 4-7)*

        1C. Its recognitions: *(vv. 4-6)*

            1D. about His providence *(v. 4)*

            2D. about His protection *(vv. 5-6)*

                1E. Manifested amidst His own *(v. 5)*

                2E. Manifested against His opponents *(v. 6)*

        2C. Its refrain *(v. 7)*

            1D. Extolling His presence *(v. 7a)*

            2D. Extolling His preservation *(v. 7b)*

    2B. The follow-up chorus of confidence about God being our Sole Resource of stability *(vv. 8-11)*

        1C. Its recognitions: *(vv. 8-10)*

            1D. call for witnessing His deeds *(vv. 8-9)*

            2D. call for worshipping Him *(v. 10)*

        2C. Its refrain *(v. 11)*

            1D. Extolling His presence *(v. 11a)*

            2D. Extolling His preservation *(v. 11b)*

Psalm 47

The two choruses of worship in Psalm 47 celebrate the universal Kingship of the LORD God Most High.

1A. The first chorus of worship is to be directed to God as *the victorious King-Warrior.* *(vv. 1-5)*

    1B. Its call to worship *(v. 1)*

        1C. Applaud Him! *(v. 1a)*

        2C. Acclaim Him! *(v. 1b)*

    2B. Its causes for worship *(vv. 2-5)*

        1C. He is Supreme. *(v. 2)*

        2C. He subjugates. *(v. 3)*

        3C. He selects. *(v. 4)*

        4C. He succeeds. *(v. 5)*

2A. The second chorus of worship is to be directed to God as *the sovereign King-Governor.* *(vv. 6-9)*

    1B. Its call to worship *(v. 6)*

    2B. Its causes for worship *(vv. 7-9b)*

        1C. His domain is universal. *(v. 7)*

        2C. His dominion is universal. *(v. 8)*

        3C. His design is universal. *(v. 9a-b)*

    3B. Its coda of worship *(v. 9c)*

Psalm 48

Psalm 48 contrasts two different responses to the God of Zion and the Zion of God.

Introduction: *(vv. 1-3)*
    The greatness of the God of Zion *(v. 1)*
    The glory of the Zion of God *(v. 2)*
    The grace of God in Zion *(v. 3)*

1A. The *panic-response* of the provokers of God *(vv. 4-7)*
    1B. The chronicling of it *(vv. 4-6)*
        1C. 'They came.' *(v. 4)*
        2C. 'They saw.' *(v. 5a)*
        3C. They <u>were</u> conquered! *(vv. 5b-6)*
    2B. The cause of it *(v. 7)*
2A. The *praise-response* of the people of God *(vv. 8-14)*
    1B. Their celebration *(vv. 8-13)*
        1C. Its promptings: *(vv. 8-9)*
            1D. a historical corroboration *(v. 8)*
            2D. a theological contemplation *(v. 9)*
        2C. Its promotions: *(vv. 10-13)*
            1D. concerning affirmation *(v. 10)*
            2D. concerning invitation:
                1E. to rejoice *(v. 11)*
                2E. to test and to testify *(vv. 12-13)*
    2B. Their conclusion *(v. 14)*

Psalm 49

The wisdom poet of Psalm 49 developed his somber theme on death as the universal experience of all men in two stages.

Introduction: *(vv. 1-4)*
His universal audience *(vv. 1-2)*
His universal teaching *(vv. 3-4)*

1A. In stage one he concentrated on *the common experience of death. (vv. 5-12)*
  1B. He first applied his teaching through an important reflection. *(vv. 5-6)*
  2B. He then explained his teaching through important reminders. *(vv. 7-12)*
    1C. No person can buy his way out of death. *(vv. 7-9)*
    2C. No person can bypass death. *(vv. 10-12)*
      1D. His reasonings *(vv. 10-11)*
      2D. His refrain *(v. 12)*
2A. In stage two he concentrated on *the contrasting experience in death. (vv. 13-20)*
    1B. The assurance of this contrasting experience in death *(vv. 13-15)*
      1C. The condemnation of the foolish *(vv. 13-14)*
      2C. The consolation of the faithful *(v. 15)*
    2B. The application of this contrasting experience in death *(vv. 16-20)*
      1C. Through his reassurance *(cf. v. 5) (v. 16)*
      2C. Through his reasonings *(cf. vv. 10-11) (vv. 17-19)*
      3C. Through his refrain *(cf. v. 12) (v. 20)*

Psalm 50

In Psalm 50, the LORD God, the Supreme Judge, levels two 'felony' charges against His professing people.

Introduction: The Supreme Judge enters to preside *(vv. 1-6)*
    The bailiff-poet's 'All Rise!' convenes the Court of the Supreme Judge. *(v. 1)*
    The bailiff-poet's video record of the Supreme Judge *(vv. 2-3)*
    The bailiff-poet's audio record of the Supreme Judge *(vv. 4-6)*

1A. The Supreme Judge first levels *the 'felony' charge of ritualism* against His professing people. *(vv. 7-16)*
    1B. His jurisdiction is affirmed. *(v.7)*
    2B. His charge is argued. *(vv. 8-13)*
    3B. His ultimatum is announced. *(vv. 14-15)*
2A. The Supreme Judge secondly levels *the 'felony' charge of rebellion* against His professing people *(vv. 16-21)*
    1B. His charge is directed. *(v. 16)*
    2B. His charge is developed. *(vv. 17-21)*

Conclusion: The Supreme Judge's final dispositions *(vv. 22-23)*
    Against rebellion *(v. 22)*
    Against ritualism *(v. 23)*

Psalm 51

Psalm 51 tracks David through three general phases in his dealing with sin before God.

1A. Phase one generally encompasses *his requests for compassion. (vv. 1-2)*
    1B. With his spotlight focusing more on God's grace *(v. 1)*
    2B. With his spotlight focusing more on his own guilt *(v. 2)*
2A. Phase two generally encompasses *his recognitions in confession. (vv. 3-5)*
    1B. With his spotlight focusing more on actual sins *(vv. 3-4)*
    2B. With his spotlight focusing more on original sin *(v. 5)*
3A. Phase three generally encompasses *his requests for consecration. (vv. 6-19)*
    1B. He first applies these requests personally. *(vv. 6-17)*
        1C. He affirms the precedent for God's consecration of him. *(v. 6)*
        2C. He alludes to the products of God's consecration of him. *(vv. 7-17)*
            1D. God's consecration would produce true sanctification in him. *(vv. 7-9)*
            2D. God's consecration would produce true service through him. *(vv. 10-13)*
            3D. God's consecration would produce true 'sacrifice' from him *(vv. 14-17)*
    2B. He finally applies these requests publicly. *(vv. 18-19)*

Psalm 52

Psalm 52 is a 'drama' about retribution and reward played out in three 'acts'.

1A. In 'act one' we view *the indictment of a snitch*. *(vv. 1-4)*
    1B. The principle undergirding this indictment:
    human bragging versus Divine blessing *(v. 1)*
    2B. The particulars unfolding this indictment *(vv. 2-4)*
        1C. The wicked calculations behind the snitch's
        communications *(v. 2)*
        2C. The wicked conduct that accompanies the snitch's
        communications *(v. 3)*
        3C. The wicked consumption that characterizes the intent of the snitch's
        communications *(v. 4)*

2A. In 'act two' we view *the intervention of the Sovereign*. *(vv. 5-7)*
    1B. The actions of God *(v. 5)*
    2B. The reactions of God's people *(vv. 6-7)*
        1C. They tremble *(v. 6a)*
        2C. They taunt *(v. 6b)*
        3C. They teach *(v. 7)*

3A. In 'act three' we view *the intentions of a servant*. *(vv. 8-9)*
    1B. The nurture behind his intentions *(v. 8a)*
    2B. The nature of his intentions *(vv. 8b-9)*
        1C. A constant faith *(v. 8b)*
        2C. A continuing praise *(v. 9a)*
        3C. A characteristic expectation *(v. 9b)*

Psalm 53

The two halves of Psalm 53 provide important Scriptural data for living wisely as rescued 'fools' among "fools."

1A. The *indicative half* contains: *(vv. 1-3)*
    1B. a brief summary of human insurrection *(v. 1)*
        1C. Its seed *(v. 1a)*
        2C. Its substance *(v. 1b)*
    2B. a brief survey of Divine investigation *(vv. 2-3)*
        1C. Its infallibility *(v.2)*
        2C. Its indications *(v. 3)*
2A. The *interactive half* connects: *(vv. 4-6)*
    1B. resistance and retribution *(vv. 4-5)*
        1C. Human resistance *(v. 4)*
        2C. Divine retribution *(v. 5)*
    2B. rescue and response *(v. 6)*
        1C. Divine rescue *(v. 6a)*
        2C. Human response *(v. 6b-c)*

Psalm 54

Once again being pursued and persecuted, David in Psalm 54 finds himself on a razor's edge between two poles of reality.

1A. The negative pole of *oppression drives him to prayer. (vv. 1-3)*

    1B. He delivers his prayers to God. *(vv. 1-2)*

        1C. 'Give me space!' *(v. 1a)*

        2C. 'Grant me justice!' *(v. 1b)*

        3C. 'Pay me attention!' *(v. 2)*

            1D. 'Hear me' *(v. 2a)*

            2D. 'Ear me' *(v. 2b)*

    2B. He documents his prayers before God. *(v. 3)*

        1C. 'I long for an answer based upon the inhumanities of my oppressors.' *(v. 3a, b)*

        2C. 'I long for an answer based upon the infidelity of my oppressors.' *(v. 3c)*

2A. The positive pole of *optimism directs him to praise. (vv. 4-7)*

    1B. The promptings of his praise *(vv. 4-5)*

        1C. Generated by God's relationship with the psalmist *(v. 4)*

        2C. Governed by God's retribution of the psalmist's enemies *(v. 5)*

    2B. The promise of his praise *(vv. 6-7)*

        1C. It will be freely delivered. *(v. 6a, b)*

        2C. It will be greatly deserved. *(vv. 6c-7)*

Psalm 55

As the persecuted poet of Psalm 55 tries to process his hurts in search of hope, three stages of emphasis progressively trace the ramblings of his thoughts.

1A. In stage one *an emphasis of reaction* best integrates his rambling thoughts. *(vv. 1-8)*

    1B. He dependently reacts to his situation with prayer. *(vv. 1-3)*

        1C. The petitions of his prayer *(vv. 1-2)*

        2C. The propriety of his prayer *(v. 3)*

    2B. He desperately reacts to his situation by dreaming about escape. *(vv. 4-8)*

        1C. His horrible anguish *(vv. 4-5)*

        2C. His human 'answer' *(vv. 6-8)*

2A. In stage two *an emphasis of retribution* best integrates his rambling thoughts. *(vv. 9-15)*

    1B. His initial request for Divine retribution *(v. 9a)*

    2B. His pertinent reasons for Divine retribution *(vv. 9b-14)*

        1C. Reasons based upon his experience with a lawless society *(vv. 9b-11)*

        2C. Reasons based upon his experience with a 'friend' turned traitor *(vv. 12-14)*

    3B. His concluding request for Divine retribution *(v. 15)*

3A. In stage three *an emphasis of relaxation* best integrates his rambling thoughts. *(vv. 16-23)*

    1B. The substance of relaxation *(vv. 16-23b)*

        1C. The learned lessons of relaxation are personally applied. *(vv. 16-21)*

            1D. Based upon his confidence in Divine compassion *(vv. 16-18)*

            2D. Based upon his confidence in Divine retribution *(vv. 19-21)*

                1E. His anticipation of retribution *(v. 19 a-b)*

                2E. His arguments for retribution *(vv. 19c-21)*

                    1F. Pertaining generally to the society *(v. 19c-d)*

                    2F. Pertaining specifically to the traitor *(vv. 20-21)*

        2C. The learned lessons of relaxation are proverbially applied. *(vv. 22-23b)*

            1D. God takes care of His own. *(v. 22)*

            2D. God 'takes care' of His opponents. *(v. 23 a-b)*

    2B. The 'signature' of relaxation *(v. 23c)*

Psalm 56

Through two choruses of complaint and confidence in Psalm 56 the psalmist exemplifies how faith operates under fire.

1A. His first chorus is ***introductory***. *(vv. 1-4)*

    1B. The complaint element of faith under fire *(vv. 1-2)*

        1C. He expresses his complaint more qualitatively *(note the generic singulars). (v. 1)*

        2C. He expresses his complaint more quantitatively *(note the concrete plurals). (v. 2)*

    2B. The confidence element of faith under fire *(vv. 3-4)*

        1C. Fear and confidence in God *(v. 3)*

        2C. Confidence in God and 'No Fear' *(v. 4)*

2A. His second chorus is ***more involved***. *(vv. 5-13)*

    1B. The complaint element of faith under fire *(vv. 5-7)*

        1C. His indictments calling for Divine judgment against his enemies *(vv. 5-6)*

        2C. His imprecations calling for Divine judgment against his enemies *(v. 7)*

    2B. The confidence element of faith under fire *(vv. 8-13)*

        1C. It is based upon God's gracious relationship with the psalmist. *(vv. 8-9)*

            1D. God's compassion is contemplated. *(v. 8)*

            2D. God's care is contemplated. *(v. 9)*

        2C. It is balanced with the psalmist's grateful responses to God. *(vv. 10-13)*

            1D. His praises and God's promise *(vv. 10-11)*

            2D. His pledges and God's preservation *(vv. 12-13)*

Psalm 57

As the psalmist practiced two primary responsibilities characteristic of all genuine disciples, he found confidence in the midst of crisis.

1A. As *he responsibly practiced prayer*, he found confidence. *(vv. 1-6)*

    1B. His prayers in a Divine context and his confidence *(vv. 1-3)*

        1C. Their expressions *(vv. 1-2)*

        2C. Their expectations *(v. 3)*

    2B. His prayers in a destructive context and his confidence *(vv. 4-6)*

        1C. The earthly reality of his prayers initially reported *(v. 4)*

        2C. The heavenly reassurance of his prayers transcendently recognized *(cf. v. 11) (v. 5)*

        3C. The earthly reality of his prayers subsequently reported *(v. 6)*

2A. As *he responsibly practiced praise*, he found confidence. *(vv. 7-11)*

    1B. His condition and praise *(v. 7a)*

    2B. His communications of praise *(vv. 7b-10)*

        1C. The resolve undergirding them *(vv. 7b-9)*

        2C. The reasons undergirding them *(v. 10)*

    3B. His content of praise *(v. 11)*

Psalm 58

Two primary forms in Psalm 58 progressively unveil the psalmist's hope that some day the scales of justice will be balanced.

1A. His *lamentations* document human injustice. *(vv. 1-5)*

   1B. He confronts unjust human leadership. *(vv. 1-2)*

   1C. Their leadership has been derelict. *(v. 1)*

   2C. Their leadership has been destructive. *(v. 2)*

   2B. He condemns unjust human leadership. *(vv. 3-5)*

   1C. By exposing their straying nature *(v. 3)*

   2C. By exposing their serpentine behavior *(vv. 4-5)*

2A. His *imprecations* desire Divine justice. *(vv. 6-11)*

   1B. Vividly expressing the intentions of his imprecations *(vv. 6-9)*

   1C. Make them toothless! *(v. 6)*

   2C. Render them powerless! *(v. 7)*

   3C. Cause them to disappear! *(v. 8)*

   4C. Do it soon! *(v. 9)*

   2B. Victoriously enjoying the fulfillment of his imprecations *(vv. 10-11)*

   1C. A personal expression of this joy *(v. 10)*

   2C. A public enhancement of this joy *(v. 11)*

Psalm 59

In Psalm 59 three poetic choruses prompted by a crisis carry the psalmist from complaint through confidence to celebration.

1A. His crisis and *his complaint (vv. 1-5)*
    1B. His enemies' injustices and his innocence
    (vv. 1-4a)
    2B. His enemies' injustices, his innocence, and God's apparent inactivity
    (vv. 4b-5)
2A. His crisis and *his confidence (vv. 6-13)*
    1B. The 'dogs' *(i.e. his enemies)* are back. *(vv. 6-7)*
    2B. But God is sovereign. *(vv. 8-13)*
        1C. An indication of His sovereignty *(v. 8)*
        2C. Some applications of His sovereignty *(vv. 9-13)*
            1D. He protects the righteous. *(vv. 9-10)*
            2D. He will punish the wicked. *(vv. 11-13)*
                1E. Phase one: Their humiliation will be a lesson for Israel.
                (v. 11)
                2E. Phase two: Their extermination will be a lesson for all.
                (vv. 12-13)
3A. His crisis and *his celebration (vv. 14-17)*
    1B. The 'dogs' are back again. *(vv. 14-15)*
    2B. But the psalmist will celebrate. *(vv. 16-17)*

Psalm 60

The abiding lesson of Psalm 60 is passed on to subsequent generations through three stages of deliberation brought on by a national disaster.

1A. The first stage of deliberation concentrates on *the agony of human defeat*. *(vv. 1-5)*
    1B. God was behind defeat. *(vv. 1-3)*
    2B. God is behind deliverance. *(vv. 4-5)*
        1C. As already demonstrated *(vv. 4-5a)*
        2C. As yet desired *(v. 5b)*
2A. The second stage of deliberation concentrates on *the assurance of Divine destinies*. *(vv. 6-8)*
    1B. God's guarantee *(v. 6a)*
    2B. God's government *(vv. 6b-8)*
        1C. His sovereignty *(vv. 6b-7)*
        2C. His subjugation *(v. 8)*
3A. The final stage of deliberation concentrates on *the awakening of human dependence*. *(vv. 9-12)*
    1B. Implied through the psalmist's questions and answers to God *(vv. 9-10)*
        1C. The inquiries *(v. 9)*
        2C. The irony *(v. 10)*
    2B. Indicated by the psalmist's final appeal to God *(vv. 11-12)*
        1C. The urgency of his appeal *(v. 11a)*
        2C. The understanding of his appeal *(vv. 11b-12)*

Psalm 61

Psalm 61 falls into two halves which worshipfully testify to Divine grace and a disciple's gratitude.

1A. The psalmist's *predicament and his prayers (vv. 1-4)*

    1B. His general invocation for a Divine audience *(v. 1)*

    2B. His particular invocations for Divine action *(vv. 2-4)*

        1C. A prayer based upon distance and need *(v. 2)*

        2C. A precedent based upon dependability in need *(v. 3)*

        3C. A prayer based upon desire and need *(v. 4)*

2A. The psalmist's *providence and his praises (vv. 5-8)*

    1B. Historically contemplated *(v. 5)*

    2B. Futuristically claimed *(i.e. by faith in God's promise) (vv. 6-7)*

        1C. The anticipated privileges *(vv. 6-7a)*

        2C. The acknowledged prerequisite *(v. 7b)*

    3B. Continuously celebrated *(v. 8)*

Psalm 62

Through three vehicles of approach, the persecuted poet of Psalm 62 practically deals with the age-old contrast between the depravity of man and the dependability of God.

1A. He first approaches this contrast through *the vehicle of trial.* *(vv. 1-4)*
    1B. His resources in God who is his Protector *(vv. 1-2)*
    2B. His responses to men who are persecutors *(vv. 3-4)*
        1C. He responds to them personally. *(v. 3)*
        2C. He responds to them publicly. *(v. 4)*
2A. He next approaches this contrast through *the vehicle of testimony.* *(vv. 5-8)*
    1B. His private testimony to himself *(vv. 5-7)*
        1C. His challenge *(v. 5a)*
        2C. His confidence *(vv. 5b-7)*
    2B. His public testimony to the community *(v. 8)*
3A. He finally approaches this contrast through *the vehicle of teaching.* *(vv. 9-12)*
    1B. His teaching about men *(vv. 9-10)*
        1C. Conveyed by weighing them *(v. 9)*
        2C. Conveyed by warning them *(v. 10)*
    2B. His teaching about God *(vv. 11-12)*
        1C. Its source *(v. 11 a-b)*
        2C. Its substance *(vv. 11c-12)*

Psalm 63

Out of the context of two relational arenas, we view the psalmist's confidence breaking through his crisis in Psalm 63.

1A. Out of *the relational arena of God and the psalmist*,
his confidence breaks through his condition. *(vv. 1-8)*

    1B. The poetic portrayal of his condition *(v. 1)*

    2B. The practical portrayal of his confidence *(vv. 2-8)*

        1C. His historical precedent *(v. 2)*

        2C. His habitual praises *(vv. 3-7)*

            1D. Generated by an enlightened perspective *(vv. 3-4)*

            2D. Fueled by a transcendent sustenance *(v. 5)*

            3D. Motivated by memory and meditation *(vv. 6-7)*

        3C. His heavenly Power-Source *(v. 8)*

            1D. Dependently affirmed *(v. 8a)*

            2D. Directly affirmed *(v. 8b)*

2A. Out of *the relational arena of God, the psalmist, and personal enemies*,
his confidence breaks through his circumstances. *(vv. 9-11)*

    1B. The crisis of his circumstances *(v. 9a)*

    2B. The contrast undergirding his confidence *(vv. 9b-11)*

        1C. The retribution of the wicked *(vv. 9b-10)*

        2C. The rewards of the worshipful *(v. 11)*

Psalm 64

Psalm 64, a story of two 'chapters' taken from real life, teaches us that God will ultimately cause the conspiracies of wicked people to boomerang on them.

1A. 'Chapter one' deals with *wicked people and their conspiracies. (vv. 1-6)*
    1B. Their effect on the righteous: a human dread which stimulates Divine dependence *(vv. 1-2)*
        1C. 'Oh God, hear me!' *(v. 1)*
        2C. 'Oh God, hide me!' *(v. 2)*
    2B. Their overt activities and underlying attitudes *(vv. 3-6)*
        1C. The focus is first on their acrimonious activities. *(vv. 3-4)*
        2C. Then the focus deepens exposing their arrogant attitudes. *(vv. 5-6)*
2A. 'Chapter two' deals with *Divine justice and counteraction (vv. 7-10)*
    1B. Its sudden execution *(vv. 7-8)*
    2B. Its immediate effects: *(vv. 9-10)*
        1C. on all who witness *(v. 9)*
        2C. on the ones who worship *(v. 10)*

Psalm 65

In Psalm 65, the psalmist crafts three Divine picture frames for his hymnic praises to God.

1A. The first Divine picture frame sets God off as *Savior.* *(vv. 1-4)*
    1B. The promise of praises *(v. 1)*
    2B. The propriety of praises *(vv. 2-4)*
        1C. You are the attentive God. *(v. 2)*
        2C. You are the pardoning God. *(v. 3)*
        3C. You are the electing God. *(v. 4)*
            1D. The blessing of election individually appreciated *(v. 4a)*
            2D. The benefit of election corporately appreciated *(v. 4b)*
2A. The second Divine picture frame sets God off as *Sovereign.* *(vv. 5-8)*
    1B. The reasons for praises *(vv. 5-7)*
        1C. God is the *sovereign* Savior. *(v. 5)*
        2C. God is the *sovereign* Creator. *(v. 6)*
        3C. God is the *sovereign* Governor. *(v. 7)*
    2B. The realms of praises *(v. 8)*
3A. The third Divine picture frame sets God off as *Sustainer.* *(vv. 9-13)*
    1B. Personal praises to the Sustainer *(vv. 9-11)*
        1C. Generally summarized *(v. 9)*
        2C. Specifically sampled *(vv. 10-11)*
            1D. Praises for rain *(v. 10)*
            2D. Praises for reaping *(v. 11)*
    2B. Personified praises to the Sustainer *(vv. 12-13)*

Psalm 66

Psalm 66 is a grand hymn which exhibits two worshipful cycles of praise and thanksgiving for God's gracious interventions.

1A. The *first cycle of praise and thanksgiving (vv. 1-7)*

    1B. It begins with an invitation to celebrate God's gracious interventions. *(vv. 1-4)*

        1C. The reverberations of celebration *(vv. 1-2)*

        2C. The reasons for celebration *(vv. 3-4)*

    2B. It ends with an invitation to contemplate God's gracious interventions. *(vv. 5-7)*

        1C. Exhortation to contemplate *(v. 5)*

        2C. Examples to contemplate *(vv. 6-7)*

2A. The *second cycle of praise and thanksgiving (vv. 8-20)*

    1B. It too begins with an invitation to celebrate God's gracious interventions. *(vv. 8-15)*

        1C. The public call to celebrate *(vv. 8-12)*

        2C. The personal commitment to celebrate *(vv. 13-15)*

    2B. It too ends with an invitation to contemplate God's gracious interventions. *(vv. 16-20)*

        1C. Exhortation to contemplate *(v. 16a)*

        2C. Experiences to contemplate *(vv. 16b-20)*

Psalm 67

Psalm 67 contains two echoing sets of longings for Israel's reception of and the world's recognition of and response to God's blessings.

*Note that the reason I speak of 'echoing sets' is because
I see evidences of a chiastic development in this Psalm.*

1A. The first set of longings includes verses 1-2 with verse 7 and involves *Israel's witness to the world* as an especially blessed people. *(vv. 1-2; v. 7)*
   1B. The sounding of this longing *(vv. 1-2)*
      1C. Its invocations *(v. 1)*
      2C. Its intentions *(v. 2)*
   2B. The echoing of this longing *(v. 7)*
      1C. Its invocation *(v. 7a)*
      2C. Its intention *(v. 7b)*
2A. The second set of longings includes verses 3-4 with verses 5-6 and involves *the world's worship* as secondarily blessed peoples. *(vv. 3-4; 5-6)*
   1B. The sounding of this longing *(vv. 3-4)*
      1C. Its responses *(vv. 3-4a)*
      2C. Its reasons *(v. 4b-c)*
         1D. The good gift of God's government *(v. 4b)*
         2D. The good gift of God's guidance *(v. 4c)*
   2B. The echoing of this longing *(vv. 5-6)*
      1C. Its responses *(v. 5)*
      2C. Its reasons *(v. 6)*
         1D. The general gift of God's produce *(v. 6a)*
         2D. The special gift of God's people *(v. 6b)*

Psalm 68

Psalm 68 is a magnificent anthem of two interrelated installments.

1A. In the first installment, God is pictured and praised as *GENERAL-King*. *(vv. 1-18)*

    1B. God, the General-King, is pictured as mustering. *(vv. 1-6)*

        1C. Against His foes *(vv. 1-2)*

        2C. For His friends *(vv. 3-6)*

    2B. God, the General-King, is pictured as marching. *(vv. 7-18)*

        1C. He exists with His people. *(vv. 7-10)*

        2C. He engages for His people. *(vv. 11-14)*

        3C. He establishes His presence. *(vv. 15-18)*

2A. In the second installment, God is pictured and praised as *KING-General*. *(vv. 19-35)*

    1B. By His nation *(vv. 19-31)*

        1C. Praising His protection *(vv. 19-23)*

        2C. Participating in His procession *(vv. 24-27)*

        3C. Previewing His prestige *(vv. 28-31)*

    2B. By all nations *(vv. 32-35)*

        1C. Exclusive of Israel *(vv. 32-34)*

        2C. Inclusive of Israel *(v. 35)*

Psalm 69

Psalm 69 is made up of two characteristically different parts.

1A. In the first part, ***the psalmist speaks out from his pain.*** *(vv. 1-29)*

> *Note that in this first part, two waves of woe tell the story of his great pain.*

    1B. The first wave washes up on the shore of invocation. *(vv. 1-18)*
        1C. His condition *(vv. 1-4)*
        2C. His confession *(v. 5)*
        3C. His community *(v. 6)*
        4C. His complaint *(vv. 7-12)*
        5C. His cries *(vv. 13-18)*
    2B. The second wave washes up on the shore of imprecation. *(vv. 19-29)*
        1C. His condition and complaint *(vv. 19-21)*
        2C. His cries *(vv. 22-28)*
        3C. His condition and confidence *(v. 29)*

2A. In the second part, ***the psalmist sings out with his praises.*** *(vv. 30-36)*
    1B. He sings a solo *(vv. 30-33)*
    2B. He leads the choirs *(vv. 34-36)*

Psalm 70

Psalm 70 is a prayer-lament tightly but carefully packaged into four circles of relational association.

1A. Its *opening invocations* are predicated upon the relational circle of God and the psalmist. *(v. 1)*

    1B. 'My God, save!' *(v. 1a)*

    2B. 'My LORD, succor!' *(v. 1b)*

2A. Its *following imprecations* are prompted by the relational circle of God and the psalmist and his enemies. *(vv. 2-3)*

    1B. 'Let their tortures bring forth Divine retributions!' *(v. 2)*

    2B. 'Let their taunts bring forth Divine retribution!' *(v. 3)*

3A. Its *subsequent intercessions* are proper for the relational circle of God and the psalmist and his community. *(v. 4)*

    1B. 'Let their obedience be worshipful!' *(v. 4a)*

    2B. 'Let their devotion be welcomed!' *(v. 4b)*

4A. Its *concluding invocations* are also *(see v. 1)* predicated upon the relational circle of God and the psalmist. *(v. 5)*

    1B. 'My God, since I am hurt, hurry up!' *(v. 5a)*

    2B. 'My LORD, since you are The Helper, hurry!' *(v. 5b)*

Psalm 71

Two rounds of reminiscence in a context of crisis fan the flames of an aging psalmist's confidence in God.

1A. In his first round of reminiscence, *he presents his prayers for rescue.* *(vv. 1-13)*

> **1B.** His opening reasons and requests for rescue: *(vv. 1-4)*
> 'Since I have been dependent *(v. 1)*, please deliver me!' *(vv. 2-4)*

> **2B.** His continuing reasons and requests for rescue: *(vv. 5-9)*
> 'Since I have been faithful *(vv. 5-8)*, please don't forget me!' *(v. 9)*

> **3B.** His culminating reasons and requests for rescue: *(vv. 10-13)*
> 'Since my enemies are vicious,*(vv. 10-11)*, please vindicate me!' *(vv. 12-13)*

2A. In his second round of reminiscence, *he promises his praises for restoration.* *(vv. 14-24)*

> **1B.** The psalmist's praises *(vv. 14-16)* and God's historic faithfulness *(vv. 17-19)*

> **2B.** God's anticipated faithfulness *(vv. 20-21)* and the psalmist's praises *(vv. 22-24)*

Psalm 72

There are three basic parts associated with Psalm 72.
> Part I: Its prayers *(vv. 1-17)*
> Part II: Its praises *(vv. 18-19)*
> Part III: Its postscript *(v. 20)*

Part I: The grand scope of the psalmist's prayers for the theocratic ruler in Psalm 72 seems to cover two domains.

1A. The psalmist's prayers for the theocratic ruler concerning
the national domain (vv. 1-7)
> **1B.** Prayers for the ethics of his reign *(vv. 1-4)*
> **2B.** Prayers for the 'economy' of his reign *(vv. 5-7)*
> *(i.e. the spiritual 'economics' of his government;*
> *cf. the more literal economic aspect in versus 16-17)*

2A. The psalmist's prayers for the theocratic ruler concerning the
international domain (vv. 8-17)
> **1B.** Prayers for the expansion of his reign *(vv. 8-15)*
>> **1C.** With a focus on geography *(vv. 8-11)*
>> **2C.** With a focus on grounds *(vv. 12-14)*
>> **3C.** With a focus on gifts *(v. 15)*
> **2B.** Prayers for the economy of his reign *(vv. 16-17)*

Part II: Its Praises *(vv. 18-19)*

Part III: Its Postscript *(v. 20)*

Psalm 73

Psalm 73 is a transparent testimony about doubt and faith poetically drawn like a circle made up of three arcs of personal experience.

This circle begins and ends with a personal conclusion for community consumption. *(v. 1)*

1A. The first arc is *a descending arc of growing consternation*
(i.e. the psalmist's faith was going down hill fast). (vv. 2-14)
    1B. His admission of envy *(vv. 2-3)*
    2B. His 'justification' with 'evidences' *(vv. 4-14)*
        1C. His initial perspective on these evidences *(vv. 4-5)*
        2C. His substantive presentation of these evidences *(vv. 6-11)*
        3C. His culminating perspective on these evidences *(vv. 12-14)*
            1D. Conquering them, the 'covenant criminals' *(v. 12)*
            2D. Concerning himself, the 'cleansed' one *(vv. 13-14)*
            (cf. the 'righteous ones' of Psalm 1)
2A. The second arc is *a bridging arc of growing contemplation and gracious confrontation*
(i.e. the psalmist's faith was turning around slowly). (vv. 15-17a)
    1B. The contemplative 'radius' of this arc *(vv. 15-16)*
    2B. The confrontational 'radius' of this arc *(v. 17a)*
3A. The third arc is *an ascending arc of growing confidence*
(i.e. the psalmist's faith was advancing steadily). (vv. 17b-28)
    1B. His confidence began to grow as he gained insight into the true existence and end of the wicked *(contra. his earlier perspective in verses 4-12). (vv. 17b-20)*
    2B. His confidence mounted as he understood more about his own relationship with the LORD. *(vv. 21-26)*
        1C. His past blindness to it *(vv. 21-22)*
        2C. His present and future blessings because of it *(vv. 23-26)*

3B. His confidence reached its zenith as he returned to reflect on the existence and ends of <u>both</u> the wicked <u>and</u> the righteous. *(vv. 27-28)*

    1C. Concerning those who are far from God *(i.e. they) (v. 27)*

    2C. Concerning the one with whom God is near *(i.e. the psalmist) (v. 28)*

    Note: Now complete the circle by going back to verse 1.

Psalm 74

The community representative of Psalm 74 puts forth his hard questions to and bold demands of the LORD God from his position of being 'trapped' between two seemingly contradictory histories.

1A. His hard questions and bold demands relate to *a current, horrible history.* *(vv. 1-11)*

> **1B.** His opening questions based upon this horrible history of recent days *(v. 1)*
>
> **2B.** His introductory demands based upon this horrible history of recent days *(vv. 2-3)*
>
> **3B.** His graphic report on this horrible history of recent days *(vv. 4-9)*
>
> **4B.** His closing questions based upon this horrible history of recent days *(vv. 10-11)*
>
> > **1C.** The 'how long?' question *(v. 10)*
> >
> > **2C.** The 'why?' question *(v. 11)*

2A. His bold demands relate to *a past, holy history. (vv. 12-23)*

> **1B.** His glowing remembrance of this holy history of days gone by *(vv. 12-17)*
>
> **2B.** His final demands based upon this holy history of days gone by *(vv. 18-23)*
>
> > **1C.** Round one of these demands *(vv. 18-21)*
> >
> > **2C.** Round two of these demands *(vv. 22-23)*

Psalm 75

Two movements in a sophisticated symphony of praises and precepts develop this psalm's major theme of retribution and reward lying exclusively in the hands of God.

1A. The first movement takes in *the many 'notes' of verses 1-8. (vv. 1-8)*
    1B. Its prelude of public praises *(v. 1)*
    2B. Its presentations of precepts *(vv. 2-8)*
        1C. Presented masterfully by God, the Divine 'Soloist' *(vv. 2-5)*
        2C. Presented meditatively by God's people, the dependent accompanists *(vv. 6-8)*
2A. The finale movement takes in *the few 'notes' of verses 9-10. (vv. 9-10)*
    1B. Its prelude of personal praises by the psalmist *(v. 9)*
    2B. Its presentation of precepts by the Divine 'Soloist' *(v. 10)*
        1C. The retribution 'notes' of His theme *(v. 10a)*
        2C. The reward 'notes' of His theme *(v. 10b)*

Psalm 76

Psalm 76 is a victory hymn of three stanzas praisefully dedicated to Yahweh-God, the incomparable Divine Warrior.

1A. In stanza one *the Divine Warrior's incomparability <u>is</u> acknowledged* among His people. *(vv. 1-3)*
    1B. The expressions of this acknowledgment *(vv. 1-2)*
    2B. The episode prompting this acknowledgment *(v. 3)*
2A. In stanza two *the Divine Warrior's incomparability <u>has been</u> demonstrated* in battle. *(vv. 4-9)*
    1B. First, with a chorus singing about the defeat of the haughty ones *(vv. 4-6)*
        1C. The theme of the singers *(v. 4)*
        2C. The triumph of the Sovereign *(vv. 5-6)*
    2B. Second, with a chorus singing about the deliverance of humbled ones *(vv. 7-9)*
        1C. The theme of the singers *(v. 7)*
        2C. The triumph of the Sovereign *(vv. 8-9)*
3A. In stanza three *the Divine Warrior's incomparability <u>will be</u> established* over all people. *(vv. 10-12)*
    1B. The certainty of its establishment *(v. 10)*
    2B. The confirmations of its establishment *(vv. 11-12)*

Psalm 77

As the author of Psalm 77 transparently testified to his turmoil, we are able to recognize two early stages in his dealings with doubt.

1A. In stage one, while he was preoccupied with self and current circumstances, we are able to recognize *an admission of doubt. (vv. 1-10)*

    1B. His requests to God brought no consolation. *(vv. 1-2)*

    2B. His reminiscences about God brought more confusion. *(vv. 3-10)*

        1C. The painful process of his reminiscences *(vv. 3-6)*

        2C. The painful questions raised by his reminiscences *(vv. 7-9)*

        3C. The painful outcome of his reminiscences *(v. 10)*

2A. In stage two, while the psalmist was preoccupied with the Sovereign and holy history, we are able to recognize *an antidote for doubt. (vv. 11-20)*

    1B. A theology of the Sovereign and holy history *(vv. 11-15)*

        1C. It launches with returning reminiscences about the Sovereign and holy history. *(vv. 11-12)*

        2C. It lands with recaptured recognitions of the Sovereign and holy history. *(vv. 13-15)*

    2B. A theophany of the Sovereign and holy history *(vv. 16-20)*

        1C. It launches with conceptualizations of the Sovereign and holy history. *(vv. 16-19)*

        2C. It lands with a conclusion about the Sovereign and holy history. *(v. 20)*

Note the rather abrupt ending of the psalm leaves the impression that there is at least one more stage in one's dealings with doubt: continuing to walk by faith in view of who God is and what He has done!

Psalm 78

The author of Psalm 78 supports the seriousness of his burden with two historical flashbacks which starkly contrast the infidelity of Israel with the fidelity of the LORD.

The introduction to his burden *(vv. 1-8)*

Part I   Pass on holy history – the obligations of testimony and tradition *(vv. 1-4)*

Part II   Pass on the Holy Scriptures including holy history – the objectives of God's Testimony and tradition *(vv. 5-8)*

1A. The first historical flashback: ***Out of Egypt and in the wilderness*** *(vv. 9-39)*

    1B. 'Chapter one' of this historical flashback *(vv. 9-16)*

        1C. Previews of the infidelity of the people *(vv. 9-11)*

        2C. Pictures of the fidelity of God *(vv. 12-16)*

            1D. The power of God in the Exodus *(vv. 12-13)*

            2D. The provisions of God in the wilderness *(vv. 14-16)*

    2B. 'Chapter two' of this historical flashback *(vv. 17-33)*

        1C. The ingratitude of the people *(vv. 17-20)*

        2C. The infuriation of God *(vv. 21-33)*

            1D. An outline of it *(vv. 21-31)*

            2D. The outcome of it *(vv. 32-33)*

                1E. Concerning the people's continuing rebellion *(v. 32)*

                2E. Concerning God's culminating retribution *(v. 33)*

    3B. 'Chapter three' of this historical flashback *(vv. 34-39)*

        1C. The people's fake repentance *(vv. 34-37)*

        2C. The LORD's faithful remission *(vv. 38-39)*

2A. The second historical flashback: ***In the wilderness and into the Promised Land*** *(vv. 40-72)*

    1B. 'Chapter one' of this historical flashback *(vv. 40-53)*

        1C. The infidelity of the people revisited *(vv. 40-42)*

        2C. The fidelity of God revisited *(vv. 43-53)*

    2B. 'Chapter two' of this historical flashback *(vv. 54-64)*

        1C. The intervention of God expanded *(vv. 54-55)*

        2C. The infidelity of the people extended *(vv. 56-57)*

        3C. The infuriation of God expressed *(vv. 58-64)*

    3B. 'Chapter three' of this historical flashback: The fidelity of God is refreshed. *(vv. 65-72)*

Psalm 79

Three form-features in Psalm 79 help to chart the course of the community's advancement from lament to laud.

1A. The psalmist begins with *the community's dirge of desperation. (vv. 1-5)*
    1B. The human instruments and the community's desperation *(vv. 1-4)*
        1C. They were instruments of desecration. *(v. 1)*
        2C. They were instruments of death. *(vv. 2-3)*
        3C. They were instruments for derision. *(v. 4)*
    2B. The Divine Instigator and the community's desperation *(v. 5)*
2A. The psalmist continues with *the community's desires for intervention. (vv. 6-12)*
    1B. Desires for retribution, focusing on death and desecration *(vv. 6-7)*
    2B. Desires for remission, focusing on: *(vv. 8-9)*
        1C. the past and the present *(v. 8)*
        2C. the present and the future *(v. 9)*
    3B. Desires for retribution, focusing on death and derision *(vv. 10-12)*
3A. The psalmist ends with *the community's dedication to devotion. (v. 13)*

Psalm 80

Psalm 80 exhibits three stanzas which develop the community's burden for the revival of the theocracy.

1A. In stanza one we find *an introduction to their burden. (vv. 1-3)*
    1B. Expressed through their general requests *(vv. 1-2)*
    2B. Expressed through their governing refrain *(v. 3)*
2A. In stanza two we feel *the intensity of their burden. (vv. 4-7)*
    1B. Expressed through their painful rejections *(vv. 4-6)*
    2B. Expressed through their passionate refrain *(v. 7)*
3A. In stanza three we follow *the impressions of their burden. (vv. 8-19)*
    1B. Expressed candidly through their reflections *(vv. 8-18)*
        1C. On their history *(vv. 8-13)*
            1D. The great 'then' *(vv. 8-11)*
            2D. The grim 'now' *(vv. 12-13)*
        2C. On their hopes: *(vv. 14-18)*
            1D. for Divine initiative *(vv. 14-17)*
            2D. for human involvement *(v. 18)*
    2B. Expressed climactically through their refrain *(v. 19)*

Psalm 81

Psalm 81 is essentially a festal sermon containing three calls.

1A. It begins with *a call to rejoice in the present.* *(vv. 1-5b)*
    1B. Built upon the people's privilege *(vv. 1-3)*
    2B. Based upon God's prescription *(vv. 4-5b)*
2A. It continues with *a call to reflect on the past.* *(vv. 5c-12)*
    1B. The 'mouth-piece' of this call to reflect *(v. 5c)*
    2B. The movements of this call to reflect *(vv. 6-12)*
        1C. The gracious intervention of God *(vv. 6-7)*
        2C. The serious instruction of God *(vv. 8-10)*
        3C. The tragic ingratitude of the people *(v. 11)*
        4C. The sobering indictment of God *(v. 12)*
3A. It concludes with *a call to repent concerning the future.* *(vv. 13-16)*
    1B. The LORD's burden *(v. 13)*
    2B. The LORD's blessings *(vv. 14-16)*

Psalm 82

Psalm 82 is a real-life vignette of three scenes which deal with the lack of and the longing for justice.

1A. In scene one *the Judge of all judges comes* to preside over them. *(v. 1)*

2A. In scene two *the Judge of all judges speaks* to arraign them. *(vv. 2-7)*

    1B. His opening interrogation *(v. 2)*

    2B. His exposing indictments *(v. 3-5)*

        1C. Broken laws are objectively resurrected. *(vv. 3-4)*

        2C. Broken laws are subjectively illustrated. *(v. 5)*

    3B. His condemning sentence *(vv. 6-7)*

        1C. Based upon their accountability *(v. 6)*

        2C. Issued in accordance with their culpability *(v. 7)*

3A. In scene three *the victims' counsel appeals* their case to the Supreme Judge. *(v. 8)*

    1B. Their counsel's plea *(v. 8a)*

    2B. Their counsel's precedent *(v. 8b)*

Psalm 83

The divinely directed poet of Psalm 83 has penned a heavy-duty song of two choruses to be sung prayerfully by Israel in times of national crisis.

1A. In the first chorus of this song, *the community in crisis sings to solicit the awareness of God. (vv. 1-8)*

    1B. In its prelude of prayer, they beg for God's awareness. *(v. 1)*

    2B. In its presentations of pressures, they bolster the need for God's awareness. *(vv. 2-8)*

        1C. The pressures produced by the arrogance of such enemies *(vv. 2-4)*

        2C. The pressures produced by the accumulation of such enemies *(vv. 5-8)*

2A. In the second chorus of this song, *the community in crisis sings to solicit the action of God. (vv. 9-18)*

    1B. Selected historical precedents for God's action *(vv. 9-12)*

    2B. Selected illustrative pictures of God's action *(vv. 13-18)*

        1C. Coming from nature in general *(vv. 13-15)*

        2C. Pertaining to human nature in particular *(vv. 16-18)*

            1D. Would that disgrace lead to devotion. *(v. 16)*

            2D. Would that devastation lead to acknowledgment. *(vv. 17-18)*

Psalm 84

As the psalmist excitedly ponders a worship-pilgrimage to God's house on Mount Zion, he mentally travels to his Divine destination through four stages of anticipation.

1A. In the first stage, *he embarks with appreciation*. *(vv. 1-4)*
    1B. His assertion of appreciation *(v. 1)*
    2B. His expressions of appreciation *(v. 2)*
    3B. His illustration of appreciation *(v. 3)*
    4B. His confirmation of appreciation *(v. 4)*
2A. In the second stage, *he contemplates the ascent*. *(vv. 5-7)*
    1B. The prerequisites for this ascent *(v. 5)*
    2B. The progress of this ascent: *(vv. 6-7)*
        1C. through the valley *(v. 6)*
        2C. to the mountain *(v. 7)*
3A. In the third stage, *he prays for acceptance*. *(vv. 8-9)*
    1B. His request *(v. 8)*
    2B. His representative *(v. 9)*
4A. In the fourth stage, *he looks forward to an entrance with adoration*. *(vv. 10-12)*
    1B. His outlook of adoration *(v. 10)*
    2B. His Object of adoration *(v. 11)*
    3B. His outburst of adoration *(v. 12)*

Psalm 85

The psalmist's three advancing perspectives on revival in Psalm 85 show his confidence in its arrival.

1A. From the perspective of *past history*, he recalls the precedent of revival.
(vv. 1-3)
    1B. It was a precedent involving Divine restoration. *(v. 1)*
    2B. It was a precedent involving Divine reconciliation. *(vv. 2-3)*
2A. From the perspective of *present history*, he responds with prayers for revival.
(vv. 4-7)
    1B. He opens his prayers with specific requests. *(v. 4)*
    2B. He supplements his prayers with pointed questions. *(vv. 5-6)*
        1C. In verse 5, his questions are phrased more negatively. *(v. 5)*
        2C. In verse 6, his questions are phrased more positively. *(v. 6)*
    3B. He closes his prayers with general requests. *(v. 7)*
3A. From the perspective of *future history*, he revels in the prospects of revival.
(vv. 8-13)
    1B. The prospect of Divine peace *(vv. 8-10)*
    2B. The prospect of Divine productivity *(vv. 11-12)*
    3B. The prospect of Divine Presence *(v. 13)*

Psalm 86

We may consider this Davidic lament as roughly falling into four sections which in combination provide a biblical perspective on tough times.

1A. The first section contains sets of *requests and reasons*. *(vv. 1-7)*

    1B. Set #1 of requests and a reason *(v. 1)*

    2B. Set #2 of a request and a reason *(v. 2a)*

    3B. Set #3 of requests and a reason *(vv. 2b-3)*

    4B. Set #4 of a request and reasons *(vv. 4-5)*

    5B. Set #5 of requests and a reason *(vv. 6-7)*

2A. The second section contains a praise-offering of *recognitions and responses*. *(vv. 8-10)*

    1B. Opening recognitions *(v. 8)*

    2B. Anticipated responses *(v. 9)*

    3B. Closing recognitions *(v. 10)*

3A. The third section contains *petitions and promises* grounded on a precedent. *(vv. 11-13)*

    1B. The petitions and promises *(vv. 11-12)*

        1C. Round one of them *(v. 11a, b)*

        2C. Round two of them *(v. 11c-12)*

    2B. The precedent *(vv. 13)*

4A. The fourth section contains some final *reasons and requests* *(note the reverse order from 1A., i.e., requests and reasons). (vv. 14-17)*

    1B. The psalmist's contrasting reasons *(vv. 14-15)*

        1C. The meanness of men *(v. 14)*

        2C. The goodness of God *(v. 15)*

    2B. The psalmist's concluding requests *(vv. 16-17)*

Psalm 87

Psalm 87 is an exuberant song of three stanzas focusing on Jerusalem, the holy city of Yahweh.

1A. The focus of verses 1-3 is upon *God's choice of the city. (vv. 1-3)*
    1B. Her establishment *(v. 1)*
    2B. Her preference *(v. 2)*
    3B. Her honor *(v. 3)*
2A. The focus of verses 4-6 is upon *God's calling of her (i.e. Zion's) citizens. (vv. 4-6)*
    1B. Their geographical distribution *(v. 4)*
    2B. Their spiritual 'domestication' *(vv. 5-6)*
3A. The focus of verse 7 is upon *her citizens' celebrations. (v. 7)*

Note some Scriptural background, terminology and theology: Genesis 12:1-3; Psalm 46:4-5; 48; 68:15-16; 76; 84; 122; 137; Isaiah 2:2-4 (cf. Micah 4:1-5); 49:14-23; 56:6-8; 66:7-14; Ezekiel 5:5; Zechariah 2:10-12; 8:22-23; John 4:22 (note the mountains-feature of this context); Ephesians 2:11-3:13; Hebrews 12:22-24; Revelation 5:9-10; 7:9-10; 21:1-3.

Psalm 88

With three outbursts of petition and plight, the psalmist speaks out from the deepest pits of human misery.

1A. His *first outburst* (*vv. 1-9a*)
    1B. His petition (*vv. 1-2*)
    2B. His plight: (*vv. 3-9a*)
        1C. personally expressed (*v. 3*)
        2C. mortally expressed (*vv. 4-5*)
        3C. theologically expressed (*vv. 6-7*)
        4C. socially expressed (*v. 8*)
        5C. weakly expressed (*v. 9a*)
2A. His *second outburst* (*vv. 9b-12*)
    1B. His petition (*v. 9b, c*)
    2B. His plight (*vv. 10-12*)
3A. His *third and final outburst* (*vv. 13-18*)
    1B. His petition (*v. 13*)
    2B. His plight (*vv. 14-18*)
        1C. He accuses God of abandoning him. (*vv. 14-15*)
        2C. He asserts that God was drowning him. (*vv. 16-17*)
        3C. He affirms that God was alienating him. (*v. 18*)

Psalm 89

In his contemplations of covenant, the perplexed author of Psalm 89 finds himself on two horns of a theological dilemma.

1A. The *first horn* is one of eternal promise and it is ***very pleasant***. *(vv. 1-37)*
    1B. This eternal promise is foundationed upon the Person of God. *(vv. 1-18)*
        1C. His greatness and goodness are revealed through individual praise. *(vv. 1-4)*
            1D. The LORD's general fidelity to covenant is praised. *(vv. 1-2)*
            2D. The LORD's specific fidelity to covenant is praised. *(vv. 3-4)*
        2C. His greatness and goodness are revealed through communal praise. *(vv. 5-14)*
            1D. Its celestial realm *(vv. 5-8)*
            2D. Its terrestrial realms *(vv. 9-14)*
        3C. His greatness and goodness are revealed through communal praise. *(vv. 15-18)*
    2B. This eternal promise unfolds in accordance with the plan of God. *(vv. 19-37)*
        1C. Looking at this plan from an unconditional vantage point *(vv. 19-29)*
            1D. The LORD's choice of "David" *(vv. 19-27)*
            2D. The LORD's perpetuation of the Davidic dynasty *(vv. 28-29)*
        2C. Looking at this plan from a complementary, not a contradictory, vantage point *(vv. 30-37)*
            1D. Its conditional vista *(vv. 30-32)*
            2D. Its unconditional vista *(vv. 33-37)*
2A. The *second horn* is one of historical prostration and it is ***very painful***. *(vv. 38-51)*
    1B. The psalmist directly recounts God's curses. *(vv. 38-45)*
    2B. The psalmist indirectly requests God's blessings. *(vv. 46-51)*
        1C. These requests are motivated by time. *(vv. 46-48)*
        2C. These requests are driven by theme. *(vv. 49-51)*

Doxology *(v. 52)*

Psalm 90

Apparently the two main divisions of Psalm 90 are designed to move the people of God from perplexity to prayer.

1A. *Some perplexities* of real life in the real world *(vv. 1-12)*
    1B. The laud which sets up these perplexities *(vv. 1-2)*
    2B. The lament which summarizes these perplexities *(vv. 3-6)*
        1C. The lament over our finiteness *(vv. 3-6)*
        2C. The lament over our fallenness *(vv. 7-11)*
    3B. The lesson surfaced by these perplexities *(v. 12)*
2A. *Sample prayers* for real life in the real world *(vv. 13-17)*
    1B. A prayer for divine restoration and 'regret' *(v. 13)*
    2B. A prayer for divine grace and gladness *(vv. 14-15)*
    3B. A prayer for divine encouragement and establishment *(vv. 16-17)*

Psalm 91

Psalm 91 contains two 'sermons' which teach and encourage the believer to keep on trusting in the LORD who alone can protect him from all kinds of dangers.

1A. The first 'sermon' comes *from the psalmist.* *(vv. 2-13)*

    1B. 'Point one' of his 'sermon': *(vv. 2-8)*

        1C. It begins with his testimony. *(v. 2)*

        2C. It continues with his teaching. *(v. 3-8)*

            1D. The LORD as a mother hen will protect you from the crafty hunter. *(vv. 3-4)*

            2D. The LORD as the Creator of light will protect you by day and by night. *(vv. 5-6)*

            3D. The LORD as the heavenly Divine Warrior will protect you in battle. *(vv. 7-8)*

    2B. 'Point two' of his 'sermon': *(vv. 9-13)*

        1C. It also begins with his testimony. *(v. 9a)*

        2C. It also continues with his teaching. *(vv. 9b-13)*

            1D. His reminder about professed dependence *(v. 9b)*

            2D. His rehearsal of protective deliverances *(vv. 10-13)*

2A. The second 'sermon' comes *from God Himself.* *(vv. 14-16)*

    1B. 'Point one' of His 'sermon': He pledges to preserve anyone who loves and respects His Person. *(v. 14)*

    2B. 'Point two' of His 'sermon': He pledges to respond to any believer who prays to Him. *(v. 15)*

    3B. 'Point three' of His 'sermon': He pledges to satiate and to save anyone who belongs to Him. *(v. 16)*

Psalm 92

Psalm 92 is a hymn of gratitude which unequally but logically falls into two main divisions.

1A. In verses 1-3, we find the psalmist's *expressions of his gratitude. (vv. 1-3)*
    1B. The attestations of his gratitude *(vv. 1-2)*
    2B. The accompaniments of his gratitude *(v. 3)*
2A. In verses 4-15, we find the psalmist's *explanations of his gratitude. (vv. 4-15)*
    1B. He first phrases these explanations antithetically.
    (vv. 4-9)
        1C. Concerning himself, the LORD brought joy to him. *(vv. 4-5)*
        2C. Concerning his God and all unrighteous people, the LORD
          will bring judgment upon them. *(vv. 6-9)*
            1D. The indictments *(vv. 5-8)*

Note that in general they have a low view of God and a high view of themselves.

            2D. The verdict and sentence *(v. 9)*
    2B. He [i.e. the psalmist] now phrases these explanations applicationally.
    (vv. 10-15)
        1C. Concerning himself,
          the LORD had given protection to him. *(vv. 10-11)*
        2C. Concerning his God and all righteous people,
          the LORD will give productivity to them. *(vv. 12-15)*
            1D. The privileges of productivity *(vv. 12-14)*
            2D. The praises for productivity *(v. 15)*

Psalm 93

Two basic biblical themes are celebrated in Psalm 93.

1A. The *supremacy of God (vv. 1-4)*
    1B. Confirmations of His supremacy are applauded. *(vv. 1-2)*
        1C. His general rule *(v. 1a, b)*
        2C. His special realm *(v. 1c)*
        3C. His eternal right *(v. 2)*
    2B. Challenges of His supremacy are acknowledged. *(vv. 3-4)*
        1C. The "'floods'" of many challenges *(v. 3)*
        2C. The frustration of all such challenges *(v. 4)*
2A. The *sufficiency of God's Word (v. 5)*
    1B. This sufficiency is affirmed. *(v. 5a)*
    2B. This sufficiency is applied. *(v. 5b, c)*

Psalm 94

In Psalm 94 the psalmist travels down four 'avenues' hoping to arrive at his 'destination' of assurance.

1A. Along the way of his first avenue, *he talks to God. (vv. 1-7)*
    1B. He prays for divine intervention. *(vv. 1-2)*
    2B. He presents his case for divine intervention: *(vv. 3-7)*
        1C. with probing questions *(v. 3)*
        2C. with powerful pieces of evidence *(vv. 4-7)*
2A. Along the way of his second avenue, *he taunts resistant people. (vv. 8-11)*
    1B. He demands their attention. *(v. 8a)*
    2B. He exposes their hardness: *(vv. 8b-11)*
        1C. with probing questions *(vv. 8b-10)*
        2C. with a powerful piece of evidence *(v. 11)*
3A. Along the way of his third avenue, *he teaches reliant people. (vv. 12-15)*
    1B. He reassures them about the mercy of God. *(vv. 12-13)*
    2B. He reminds them about the justice of God. *(vv. 14-15)*
4A. Along the way of his fourth avenue, *he testifies to God's provisions.*
    1B. The precedent of God's past provisions. *(vv. 16-23)*
        1C. The psalmist's questions imtimate that God
        is his Advocate. *(v. 16)*
        2C. The psalmist's concluding observations confirm that God
        is his Sustainer. *(vv. 17-19)*
        3C. The psalmist's concluding observations confirm that God
        is his Protector. *(vv. 20-22)*
    2B. The promise of God's future provisions. *(v. 23)*

Psalm 95

Psalm 95 contains two common elements of Israel's liturgy which are generally applicable to our worship today.

1A. The *summons to celebrate* *(vv. 1-7b)*
    1B. The initial stage of this summons to celebrate *(vv. 1-5)*
        1C. The exhortations of this initial stage *(vv. 1-2)*
        2C. The explanations of this initial stage *(vv. 3-5)*
    2B. The intimacy state of this summons to celebrate *(vv. 6-7b)*
        1C. The exhortations of this initial stage *(v. 6)*
        2C. The explanations of this initial stage *(v. 7a, b)*
2A. The *sermon to contemplate* *(vv. 7c-11)*
    1B. Its present application *(v. 7c)*
    2B. Its probing prohibition *(v. 8a)*
    3B. Its pertinent illustration *(vv. 8b-11)*
        1C. The people's resistance *(vv. 8b-9)*
        2C. The LORD's response *(vv. 10-11)*
            1D. His rejection of them *(v. 10)*
            2D. His retribution of them *(v. 11)*

Psalm 96

Psalm 96 contains three intensifying and widening calls to the praise of Yahweh, the only true God.

1A. The community is called upon to *praise Him as Savior and Creator. (vv. 1-6)*
    1B. Appropriate responses of the community's praise *(vv. 1-3)*
        1C. The response of worship *(vv. 1-2a)*
        2C. The response of witness *(vv. 2b-3)*
    2B. Attendant reasons for the community's praise *(vv. 4-6)*
        1C. His supremacy *(vv. 4-5)*
        2C. His superiority *(v. 6)*
2A. The clans are called upon to *praise Him as ruling Sovereign. (vv. 7-10)*
    1B. The response of worship *(vv. 7-9)*
    2B. The response of witness *(v. 10)*
3A. The creation is called upon to *praise Him as imminent Judge. (vv. 11-13)*
    1B. Appropriate responses of the creation's praise *(vv. 11-13a)*
    2B. Attendant reasons for the creation's praise *(v. 13b-d)*

Psalm 97

Psalm 97 is a majestic poetic symphony of three themes on Divine revelations and creaturely responses.

1A. The first theme contains *universal responses to revelations of Yahweh's awesome sovereignty. (vv. 1-6)*

    1B. This theme on sovereignty commences with universal responses of joy. *(v. 1)*

    2B. This theme on sovereignty continues with revelations of Yahweh's terrorizing presence. *(vv. 2-4a)*

    3B. This theme on sovereignty concludes with universal responses of submission: *(vv. 4b-6)*

        1C. poetically pictured *(vv. 4b-5)*

        2C. personally proclaimed *(v. 6)*

2A. The second theme contains *peoples' responses to revelations of Yahweh's absolute supremacy. (vv. 7-9)*

    1B. Some contrasting responses of people: *(vv. 7-8)*

        1C. fitting responses from pagan peoples *(v. 7)*

        2C. fitting responses from Yahweh's people *(v. 8)*

    2B. Some causative revelations of Yahweh's exalted position *(v. 9)*

3A. The third theme contains *disciples' responses to revelations of Yahweh's amazing salvation. (vv. 10-12)*

    1B. This theme on salvation commences with disciples' contrasting responses of love and hate. *(v. 10a)*

    2B. This theme on salvation continues with revelations of Yahweh's merciful care. *(vv. 10b-11)*

    3B. This theme on salvation concludes with disciples' celebratory responses of joy and praise. *(v. 12)*

Psalm 98

In Psalm 98 the psalmist leads three enlarging choirs in praise of the Divine Warrior who is cast in His major roles.

1A. In verses 1-3 the psalmist leads *the choir of Israel in praise of the Divine Warrior-Savior. (vv. 1-3)*
    1B. The direction to Israel to express their praises *(v. 1a)*
    2B. The documentation for Israel about the Divine Warrior's salvation *(1b-3)*
        1C. The fact of His saving victories *(1b, c)*
        2C. The exhibition of His saving victories *(vv. 2, 3b)*
        3C. The beneficiary of his saving victories *(v. 3a)*
2A. In verses 4-6 the psalmist leads *the choir of all people in praise of the Divine Warrior-King. (vv. 4-6)*
    1B. He directs their vocal praises in recognition of the Great King. *(v. 4)*
    2B. He directs their vocal and instrumental praises in recognition of the Great King. *(vv. 5-6)*
        1C. Praises accompanied by stringed instruments *(v. 5)*
        2C. Praises accompanied by wind instruments *(v. 6)*
3A. In verses 7-9 the psalmist leads *the choir of all nature in praise of the Divine Warrior-Judge. (vv. 7-9)*
    1B. The direction to all nature to express praises *(vv. 7-9a)*
        1C. Praises of the sea *(v. 7a)*
        2C. Praises of the land *(vv. 7b-9a)*
    2B. The documentation for all nature about the Divine Warrior's Justice *(v. 9b-d)*

Psalm 99

Psalm 99 contains three stanzas of recognitions, responses, and a common refrain on the sanctity of the LORD.

1A. The first stanza is *universal in Scope* and focuses on *the LORD's supremacy.* (*vv. 1-3*)

    1B. The recognitions of His supremacy (*vv. 1a, c; 2*)

    2B. The responses to His supremacy (*vv. 1b, d; 3a*)

    3B. The refrain applied to His supremacy (*v. 3b*)

2A. The second stanza is *national in scope* and focuses on *the LORD's justice.* (*vv. 4-5*)

    1B. The recognitions of His justice (*v. 4*)

    2B. The responses to His justice (*v. 5a, b*)

    3B. The refrain applied to His justice (*v. 5c*)

3A. The third stanza is *national in scope* and focuses on *the LORD's grace.* (*vv. 6-9*)

    1B. The recognitions of His grace (*vv. 6-8*)

    2B. The responses to His grace (*v. 9a, b*)

    3B. The refrain applied to His grace (*v. 9c*)

Psalm 100

The two basic parts of Psalm 100 constitute Israel's call for the universal praise of Yahweh.

1A. In part one Israel puts forth her *commands to praise the LORD. (vv. 1-4)*
    1B. Her command to acclaim Him vocally *(v. 1)*
    2B. Her command to worship Him practically *(v. 2a)*
    3B. Her command to approach him enthusiastically *(v. 2b)*
    4B. Her command to acknowledge Him exclusively *(v. 3)*
        1C. The statement of it *(v. 3a)*
        2C. The support of it *(v. 3b)*
    5B. Her command to come into His presence gratefully *(v. 4a, b)*
    6B. Her command to thank Him personally *(v. 4c)*
    7B. Her command to praise Him corporately *(v. 4d)*
2A. In part two Israel publishes her *causes for praising the LORD. (v. 5a)*
    1B. The LORD God is supremely beneficent. *(v. 5a)*
    2B. The LORD God is forever loyal. *(v. 5b)*
    3B. The LORD God is always reliable. *(v. 5c)*

Psalm 101

Psalm 101 contains three different kinds of statements relating to the commitments of a theocratic king to a God-honoring administration.

1A. He begins with *a statement of praise. (v. 1)*
2A. He slips in *a statement of perplexity. (v. 2b)*
3A. He continues and concludes with *statements of pledge or practice. (vv. 2a, c-8)*
    1B. Pertaining to himself personally *(vv. 2a, c-4)*
        1C. What he resolves *(v. 2a, c)*
        2C. What he rules out *(vv. 3-4)*
    2B. Pertaining to his reign administratively *(vv. 5-8)*
        1C. Illustrated by those he rejects *(vv. 5, 7-8)*
        2C. Illustrated by those he recognizes *(v. 6)*

Psalm 102

As the Psalmist contemplates a great crisis out of the contexts of various relational associations and time frames, we are able to witness his three developing outlooks.

1A. From the intimate context of God and himself at present time, the psalmist's outlook is *quite pessimistic. (v. 1-11)*

    1B. The urgency of his prayers sets the stage for his pessimistic outlook. *(vv. 1-2)*

    2B. The description of his condition helps to explain his pessimistic outlook. *(vv. 3-11)*

        1C. He felt like his distress was dehydrating him spiritually. *(vv. 3-5)*

        2C. He felt like his situation was isolating him socially. *(vv. 6-7)*

        3C. He felt like he was being victimized unsparingly. *(vv. 8-11)*

            1D. The ridicule of his enemies *(vv. 8-9)*

            2D. The retribution of his God *(vv. 10-11)*

2A. From the covenantal context of God and His people in future time, the psalmist's outlook is *very optimistic. (v. 12-22)*

    1B. The promise of future divine blessing *(vv. 12-17)*

    2B. The future publication of that divine blessing. *(vv. 18-22)*

3A. From the largest context of God, Himself, and future generations, looking both at the present and then to the future, the Psalmist's outlook is *more realistic. (vv. 23-28)*

    1B. His crisis reviewed *(vv. 23-27)*

    2B. His confidence renewed. *(v. 28)*

Notice once again the sharp contrast between the existence of men and the existence of God.

Psalm 103

Psalm 103 is a grand hymn of praise to the LORD, especially for the underserved grace that He grants to sinful human beings. In this awesome anthem of worship, the Psalmist directs three enlarging choirs of praise to God.

1A. In the opening of this hymn, he directs the 'choir' of *his inner being* to praise the LORD *(i.e. the psalm begins with a personal 'solo' of the heart; the psalm will also end on this note in v. 22c). (vv. 1-5)*

    1B. The Psalmist's personal directives *(vv. 1-2)*

    2B. The Psalmist's personal documentation *(vv. 3-5)*

2A. In the core of this hymn, he directs the choir of *the community* of all God-fearers to praise the LORD. *(vv. 6-18)*

    1B. This praise is based upon the precedent of God's historical mercy. *(vv. 6-8)*

    2B. This praise is based upon the promise of continuing mercy. *(vv. 9-18)*

        1C. This promise is related to our Divine Judge's forgiveness. *(vv. 9-12)*

        2C. This promise is related to our Divine Father's forbearance. *(vv. 13-18)*

3A. In the finale of this hymn, he directs the choir of *the universe* to praise the LORD. *(vv. 19-22)*

    1B. His documentation for universal praise *(v. 19)*

    2B. His directives for universal praise *(v. 20-21)*

        1C. First given to the holy angels *(vv. 20-21)*

        2C. Then given to the rest of creation *(v. 22a, b)*

        3C. Finally given to himself once again *(v. 22c)*

Psalm 104

In Psalm 104, the Psalmist's calls to praise the LORD bookend his two main arguments for doing so.

His Opening Call to Praise *(v. 1a)*

1A. The Psalmist's first argument is that the LORD deserves all praises because He is the ***Great Creator.*** *(vv. 1b-9)*
    1B. The poetic pictures of His heavenly creation *(vv. 1b-4)*
    2B. The poetic pictures of His earthly creation *(vv. 5-9)*
2A. The Psalmist's second argument is that the LORD deserves all praises because He is the ***Great Sustainer.*** *(vv. 10-30)*
    1B. He waters all creation. *(vv. 10-13)*
    2B. He feeds and 'houses' all His creatures. *(vv. 14-18)*
    3B. He 'schedules' all creation. *(vv. 19-23)*
    4B. He 'adds to' and 'subtracts from' His creatures. *(vv. 24-30)*

His Closing Call to Praise *(vv. 31-35)*

Psalm 105

Psalm 105 focuses on the faithful LORD of salvation history. The psalm divides into two parts, and throughout both of these parts the worship leader prompts the people to praise their God.

1A. In part one the Psalmist calls upon his community to revere *the God who acts*. *(vv. 1-6)*

> **1B.** They are called upon to praise and publish Him. *(vv. 1-2)*
> **2B.** They are called upon to praise and pursue Him. *(vv. 3-4)*
> **3B.** They are called upon to praise Him by pondering His works. *(vv. 5-6)*

> *Note: Verses 5-6 build a bridge to the second part of this psalm.*

2A. In part two the Psalmist calls upon his community to reflect on *the acts of God*. *(vv. 7-45)*

> **1B.** They are called upon to reflect on the scope of God's acts. *(vv. 7)*
> **2B.** They are called upon to reflect on the basis of God's acts:
> The covenant promises made to the patriarchs. *(8-15)*
> **3B.** They are called upon to reflect on some samples of God's acts. *(vv. 16-45)*
>> **1C.** Relating to the protection of His people in exile
>> *(vv. 16-36)*
>>> **1D.** Protection from starvation *(vv. 16-24)*
>>> **2D.** Protection from slaughter *(vv. 25-36)*
>> **2C.** Relating to the provisions for His people throughout the exodus
>> *(vv. 37-45)*
>>> **1D.** Selected indications of His provisions *(vv. 37-44)*
>>> **2D.** Selected intentions concerning His provisions. *(v. 45)*
>>>> **1E.** Practical worship *(v. 45a, b)*
>>>> **2E.** Public worship *(v. 45c)*

Psalm 106

The basic structure of this psalm is as follows:

Introduction: Praise and Prayer *(vv. 1-5)*

Central Core: Cycles of Israel's unfaithfulness and their God's faithfulness *(vv. 6-46)*

Conclusion: Prayer and Praise *(vv. 47-48)*

In the massive core of Psalm 106, the Psalmist selects illustrative episodes from three eras of salvation history in order to paint a picture of the amazing mercy of God on the black canvas of the mutinies of His professing people.

Introduction *(vv. 1-5)*

Corporate praise is enjoined. *(vv. 1-3)*

Personal prayers are added. *(vv. 4-5)*

Central Core *(vv. 6-46)*

1A. The first era of salvation history takes in *the Exodus from Egypt. (vv. 6-12)*

  1B. The Psalmist begins with a clarification: when it comes to unfaithfulness, we and our fathers are in the same boat. *(v. 6)*

  2B. The Psalmist continues with a cycle: *(vv. 7-12)*

    1C. the rebellion of the people *(vv. 7)*

    2C. the response of their God *(v. 8-11)*

    3C. the repentance of the people *(v. 12)*

2A. The second era of salvation history takes in *the wilderness wanderings. (vv. 13-15)*

  1B. The episode of craving meat *(vv. 14-15)*

  2B. The episode of jealousy of God's appointed leaders *(vv. 16-18)*

  3B. The episode of wanton idolatry *(vv. 19-23)*

    1C. The mutiny of the people *(vv. 19-22)*

    2C. The mediation of Moses *(v. 23)*

  4B. The episode of 'being chicken' about taking the Promised Land *(vv. 24-27)*

    1C. The reactions of the people *(vv. 24-25)*

    2C. The response of God *(vv. 26-27)*

5B. The episode of Moabite pollutions *(vv. 28-31)*

    1C. The insurrections of the people *(v. 28)*

    2C. The judgment of God *(v. 29)*

    3C. The intervention of Phinehas *(vv. 30-31)*

6B. The episode of contending about water *(vv. 32-33)*

3A. The third era of salvation history takes in a long period from *the conquest to captivity and beyond. (vv. 34-46)*

    1B. The people's disobedience in the land *(vv. 34-39)*

    2B. The LORD's responses *(vv. 40-46)*

        1C. His righteous responses *(vv. 40-43)*

        2C. His compassionate responses *(vv. 44-46)*

Conclusion *(vv. 47-48)*

    Corporate prayers *(v. 47)*

    Corporate praises *(v. 48)*

Psalm 107

The Spirit-directed writer of Psalm 107 delivers two motivational messages to the LORD's people.

1A. In *vv.* 1-32 the Psalmist urges the people of God *to praise the LORD for His patience. (vv. 1-32)*

    1B. His call to praise *(vv. 1-3)*

    2B. His sample scenarios for praise: *(vv. 4-32)*

        Note the four cycles of peril, prayer, provision, and praise in these verses.

        1C. Recognizing human deprivation, the LORD responds to the prayers of people in need. *(vv. 4-9)*

        2C. In spite of human rejection, the LORD rescues repentant rebels. *(vv. 10-16)*

        3C. In spite of human resistance, the LORD rescues penitent petitioners. *(vv. 17-22)*

        4C. Caring about human crises, the LORD responds to the prayers of people in peril. *(vv. 23-32)*

2A. In verses 33-43 the Psalmist urges the people of God to *ponder the LORD's sovereign providence. (vv. 33-43)*

    1B. His sample scenarios for pondering the LORD's sovereign providence *(vv. 33-42)*

        1C. The scenario from the arena of 'nature' *(vv. 33-38)*

            1D. The heavy-duty side of the LORD's sovereign providence in the arena of 'nature' *(vv. 33-34)*

            2D. The brighter side of the LORD's sovereign providence in the arena of 'nature' *(vv. 35-38)*

        2C. The scenario form the arena of salvation history *(vv. 39-40)*

            1D. The heavy-duty side of the LORD's sovereign providence in the arena of salvation history *(vv. 39-40)*

            2D. The brighter side of the LORD's sovereign providence in the arena of salvation history *(vv. 41-42)*

    2B. His call to ponder the LORD's sovereign providence *(v. 43)*

Psalm 108

The composer of Psalm 108 selected two portions from previous Davidic psalms and combined them into a modern medley which spoke authoritatively and applicationally to the people of his day.

1A. In verses 1-5 he selected a portion from Psalm 57 *(i.e. vv. 7-11) to express his personal confidence with praise. (vv. 1-5)*

    1B. His trust *(v. 1a)*

    2B. His 'tune' *(vv. 1b-5)*

2A. In verses 6-13 he selected a portion from Psalm 60 *(i.e. vv. 5-12) to express his community's crisis with prayer. (vv. 6-13)*

    1B. The 'target' of his prayer *(v. 6)*

    2B. The theology of his prayer *(vv. 7-13)*

        1C. Supported by promises *(vv. 7-9)*

        2C. Clouded by circumstance *(vv. 10-11)*

        3C. Cleared up by confidence *(vv. 12-13)*

Psalm 109

The intensity of emotion in this psalm is overwhelming. The Psalmist's pain is of the most crushing variety: he is being unjustly persecuted.

As we listen to this psalmist's agonizing outbursts, they seem to fall logically into three categories.

1A. His outbursts in verses 1-5 fall into the category of *injustices*. *(vv. 1-5)*

    1B. The appeal to the Divine Judge concerning the injustices of his enemies *(v. 1)*

    2B. The arraignment before the Divine Judge concerning the injustices of his enemies *(vv. 2-5)*

2A. His outbursts in verses 6-20 fall into the category of *imprecations*. *(vv. 6-20)*

    1B. His specific imprecations: *(vv. 6-19)*

        1C. concerning the trial of his enemy(ies) *(vv. 6-7)*

        2C. concerning the life-span of his enemy(ies) *(vv. 8-9)*

        3C. concerning the progeny and prosperity of his enemy(ies) *(vv. 10-13)*

        4C. concerning the ancestry of his enemy(ies) *(vv. 14-16)*

        5C. concerning the exact requital of his enemy(ies) *(vv. 17-19)*

    2B. His summary of these imprecations *(v. 20)*

3A. His outbursts in verses 21-31 fall into the category of *invocations*. *(vv. 21-31)*

    1B. The expressions of these invocations *(vv. 21-29)*

        1C. His first installment *(vv. 21-25)*

        2C. His final installment *(vv. 26-29)*

    2B. The hope of these invocations *(vv. 30-31)*

Psalm 110

David functions like a prophet in Psalm 110 in that he receives and passes on Divine revelation. To be specific, the Spirit of God moves him to record two important oracles about Messiah.

1A. The first oracle majestically pictures Messiah as ***the King-Warrior***. *(vv. 1-3)*

    1B. The affirmations of this oracle about Messiah as King-Warrior *(vv. 1-2)*

        1C. Concerning Messiah's position *(v. 1)*

        2C. Concerning Messiah's power *(v. 2)*

    2B. The confirmations of this oracle about Messiah as the King-Warrior *(v. 3)*

        1C. This oracle is confirmed by the nature of Messiah's military forces. *(v. 3a)*

        2C. This oracle is also confirmed by the number of Messiah's military forces. *(v. 3b, c)*

2A. The second oracle marvelously pictures Messiah as ***the Priest-Warrior***. *(vv. 4-7)*

    1B. The affirmation of this oracle about Messiah as Priest-Warrior *(v. 4)*

    2B. The confirmations of this oracle about Messiah as Priest-Warrior *(vv. 5-7)*

        1C. This oracle is confirmed by the position of Messiah. *(v. 5a)*

        2C. This oracle is confirmed by the power of Messiah. *(vv. 5b-6)*

        3C. This oracle is confirmed by the pre-eminence of Messiah. *(v. 7)*

Psalm 111

In Psalm 111 motivation for public and private worship is generated by four cycles of deductions which flow from a contemplation of divine deeds.

Introduction: The Psalm opens with a Call to Public Worship. *(v. 1)*
  The Role of the Community
  The Role of the Individual

1A. The 1st Cycle of Deductions is ***comprehensive*** and therefore the ***most general.*** *(vv. 2-3)*
  1B. Deductions about Divine deeds *(vv 2-3a)*
    1C. Quantitatively, they are multitudinous. *(v. 2a)*
    2C. Applicationally, they are memorable. *(v. 2b)*
    3C. Qualitatively, they are magnificent. *(v. 3a)*
  2B. A deduction about Divine dignity *(v. 3b)*
2A. The 2nd Cycle of Deductions is ***liturgical*** and therefore the ***most focused.*** *(v. 4)*
  1B. The Divine deed *(v. 4a)*
  2B. The derived deduction *(v. 4b)*
3A. The 3rd Cycle of Deductions is ***illustrative*** and therefore the ***most historical.*** *(vv. 5-8)*
  1B. Illustrated deeds: *(vv. 5-6)*
    1C. the refreshment of the LORD *(v. 5a)*
    2C. the remembrance of the LORD *(v. 5b)*
    3C. the revelation of the LORD *(v. 6)*
  2B. Interrelated deductions: *(vv. 7-8)*
    1C. concerning the <u>works</u> of God *(v. 7a)*
    2C. concerning the words (i.e. <u>Word</u>) of God: *(vv. 7b-8)*
      1D. They are inherently dependable. *(v. 7b)*
      2D. They are constantly upheld. *(v. 8a)*
      3D. They are perfectly applied. *(v. 8b)*

4A. The 4th and final Cycle of Deductions is *redemptive* and therefore the
most intimate. *(v. 9)*

    1B. Final deeds: *(v. 9a, b)*

        1C. the LORD's performance with an emphasis
upon His provision *(v. 9a)*

        2C. the LORD's performance with an emphasis
upon His plan *(v. 9b)*

    2B. Final deductions: *(v. 9c)*

        1C. the LORD's Person with a comparative emphasis
upon His sanctity

        2C. the LORD's Person with an applicational emphasis
upon His awesomeness

Conclusion: The Psalm closes with a Concern for Private Worship. *(v. 10)*

    Its Prerequisite

    Its Practicality

    Its Perpetuity

Psalm 112

The theme of the respect and the rewards of godly people is developed in two ways in Psalm 112.

A Worshipful Introduction: Praising the God of godly people. *(v. 1a)*

1A. This theme is first developed *by way of characteristics. (vv. 1b-9)*
    1B. An initial consideration of their characteristics *(vv. 1b-6)*
        1C. Godly people are characterized by fear and fervency. *(v. 1b, c)*
        2C. Godly people are characterized by reputation and richness. *(vv. 2-3)*
        3C. Godly people are characterized by hope and help. *(vv. 4-6)*
    2B. A follow-up consideration of their characteristics *(vv. 7-9)*
        1C. Godly people are characterized by "'no fear'" and faith. *(vv. 7-8)*
        2C. Godly people are characterized by benevolence and blessing. *(v. 9)*
2A. This theme is finally developed *by way of contrast. (v. 10)*
    1B. Wicked people will be frustrated. *(v. 10 a, b)*
    2B. Wicked peoples' wills and ways will be finished. *(v. 10c)*

Psalm 113

In Psalm 113 genuine thanksgiving should be promoted by our contemplation of two general attributes of God.

1A. His *greatness* should prompt genuine thanksgiving. *(vv. 1-4)*
    1B. Our response to His attribute of greatness *(vv. 1-3)*
        1C. Its expression *(v. 1)*
        2C. Its extent: *(vv. 2-3)*
            1D. from ever and always (time*) (v. 2)*
            2D. from East to West (space*) (v. 3)*
    2B. Our recognition of His attribute of greatness *(v. 4)*
2A. His *goodness* should prompt genuine thanksgiving. *(vv. 5-9)*
    1B. Our recognition of His attribute of goodness *(vv. 5-9b)*
        1C. His attribute of goodness is first explained; perfect balance: *(vv. 5-6)*
            1D. the compatibility of His goodness in view of His greatness *(v. 5)*
            2D. the compassion of His goodness in view of His greatness *(v. 6)*
        2C. His attribute of goodness is then illustrated: *(vv. 7-9b)*
            1D. His concern and care for the downtrodden *(vv. 7-8)*
            2D. His concern and care for the childless *(v. 9a-b)*
    2B. Our response to His attribute of goodness *(v. 9c)*

Psalm 114

Structurally Psalm 114 is made up of four pairs of verses with each verse containing two lines. The middle two pairs of verses are highly poetic and are intimately related by a four-line sequence which is repeated (i.e. "sea," "Jordan," "mountains, "hills"). Therefore, logically the psalmist seems to be arranging these parts climactically into a three-point 'sermon.'

1A. In 'point one' *he identifies an important historical event. (vv. 1-2)*
    1B. Its occurrence *(v. 1)*
    2B. Its outcome *(v. 2)*
2A. In 'point two' *he dramatizes that event*
with a poetic explanation: *(vv. 3-6)*

        Note that this is the 'stuff' of theophanies.

    1B. via personifications *(vv. 3-4)*
    2B. via rhetorical questions *(vv. 5-6)*

3A. In 'point three' *he applies that event* and its poetic explanation
with a contemporary exhortation. *(vv. 7-8)*

Psalm 115

The two conflicting theologies outlined in the core of Psalm 115 are skillfully employed by the psalmist to prompt the people of God to praise their Living LORD.

The Praise-Preface to these theologies prompts praise. *(vv. 1-3)*

1A. The *tragic theology of idolatry (vv. 4-8)*
    1B. Its stupidity *(vv. 4-7)*
    2B. Its sadness *(v. 8)*
2A. The *true theology of Israel (vv. 9-16)*
    1B. Its faith in the Living God *(vv. 9-11)*
    2B. Its hope in the Living God *(vv. 12-16)*

The Praise-Conclusion to these theologies also prompts praise. *(vv. 17-18)*

Psalm 116

In Psalm 116 its grateful author employs two means to motivate his community to follow him in worship.

1A. By means of a personal testimony about answered prayer, he exemplifies *a proper attitude for worship. (vv. 1-11)*

    1B. He first outlines his testimony about answered prayer. *(vv. 1-4)*

        1C. The principles learned from it *(vv. 1-2)*

        2C. The process leading up to it *(vv. 3-4)*

    2B. He next expands his testimony about answered prayer. *(vv. 5-11)*

        1C. More of the principles learned from it *(vv. 5-9)*

        2C. More about the process leading up to it *(vv. 10-11)*

2A. By means of a personal tribute based upon answered prayer, he exemplifies *some proper activities in worship. (vv. 12-19)*

    1B. He first outlines his tribute based upon answered prayer. *(vv. 12-14)*

        1C. His tribute is prompted by contemplation. *(v. 12)*

        2C. His tribute is published with celebration. *(vv. 13-14)*

    2B. He next expands his tribute based upon answered prayer. *(vv. 15-19)*

        1C. His tribute is again prompted by contemplation. *(vv. 15-16)*

        2C. His tribute is again published with celebration. *(vv. 17-19)*

Psalm 117

This mini but magnificent symphony of praise evidences three celebratory movements.

1A. Its introductory movement contains *an initial summons to universal praise. (v. 1)*
>   **1B.** Expressed nationally *(v. 1a)*
>   **2B.** Expressed ethnically *(v. 1b)*

2A. Its middle movement contains *motives for universal praise. (v. 2a, b)*
>   **1B.** The proven loyalty of the LORD *(v. 2a)*
>   **2B.** The eternal fidelity of the LORD *(v. 2b)*

3A. Its final movement contains *a concluding summons to universal praise. (v. 2c)*

Psalm 118

Psalm 118 is a hymn of thanksgiving sung by various worshippers on the move. As we trace their movement, we also note that this liturgical laud is offered up to God from two locations.

1A. They commence their liturgical laud by
   worshipping God along the way to His house. (vv. 1-18)
   1B. Their prelude of praise *(vv. 1-4)*
      1C. The call to praise *(v. 1a)*
      2C. The chorus of praise *(vv. 1b-4)*
   2B. Their leader's testimony of praise *(vv. 5-18)*
      1C. He begins this testimony with a thumb-nail sketch of his distress and deliverance. *(v. 5)*
      2C. He continues this testimony with an expanded picture of his distress and deliverance. *(vv. 6-16)*
         1D. Emphasizing his dependence upon God *(vv. 6-13)*
         2D. Emphasizing his victory through God *(vv. 14-16)*
      3C. He concludes this testimony with a condensed summary of his distress and deliverance. *(vv. 17-18)*

2A. They continue their liturgical laud by
   worshipping God in His house. (vv. 19-20)
   1B. The request and response to enter God's house *(vv. 19-20)*
   2B. The diversity and dynamic of worship in God's house *(vv. 21-29)*
      1C. The leader sets the pace. *(v. 21)*
      2C. The whole assembly joins in. *(vv. 22-27)*
         1D. With joyous acknowledgment *(vv. 22-24)*
         2D. With fervent prayers *(v. 25)*
         3D. With priestly pronouncements *(vv. 26-27)*
      3C. The leader brings the worship to its climax. *(vv. 28-29)*
         1D. By singing a final solo *(v. 28)*
         2D. By directing the grand finale *(v. 29)*

Psalm 119

Aleph

In this first stanza of Psalm 119 it foundationally emphasizes three interrelated perspectives on the priority of obedience.

1A. *The perspective of all the faithful* on the priority of obedience *(vv. 1-3)*
    1B. They experience the happiness of obedience. *(vv. 1-2)*
        1C. This happiness comes from conformity to God's Word. *(v. 1)*
        2C. This happiness comes from knowing God through His Word. *(v. 2)*
            1D. Knowing the Word of God *(v. 2a)*
            2D. Knowing the God of the Word *(v. 2b)*
    2B. They experience the practicality of obedience. *(v. 3)*
        1C. This practicality is first expressed negatively. *(v. 3a)*
        2C. This practicality is then expressed positively. *(v. 3b)*
2A. *The perspective of God* on the priority of obedience *(v. 4)*
    1B. His standard concerning obedience *(v. 4a)*
    2B. His burden concerning obedience *(v. 4b)*
3A. *The perspective of the psalmist* on the priority of obedience *(vv. 5-8)*
    1B. His positively phrased plea for enablement points to the priority of obedience. *(vv. 5-8a)*
        1C. The potential of this plea for enablement *(v. 5)*
        2C. The products of this plea for enablement: *(vv. 6-8a)*
            1D. the immediate product: maturing integrity *(v. 6)*
            2D. the related products: *(vv. 7-8a)*
                1E. formal worship *(v. 7)*
                2E. practical worship *(v. 8a)*
    2B. His negatively phrased plea for communion points to the priority of obedience. *(v. 8b)*

Psalm 119

ב

Beth

Psalm 119:9-16 presents three crucial ingredients in reference to personal sanctification.

1A. The first ingredient: *the right attitude* (*vv. 9-11*)

    1B. It is an attitude characterized by awareness. (*v. 9*)

    2B. It is an attitude characterized by acknowledgment. (*v. 10*)

        1C. A crucial acknowledgement of the God of the Word (*v. 10a*)

        2C. A crucial acknowledgment of the Word of God (*v. 10b*)

    3B. It is an attitude characterized by accrual. (*v. 11*)

        1C. The testimony of this accrual (*v. 11a*)

        2C. The target of this accrual (*v. 11b*)

2A. The second ingredient: *the right Source (i.e. God)* (*v. 12*)

    1B. The character of this Source (*v. 12a*)

    2B. The capability of this Source (*v. 12b*)

3A. The third ingredient: *the right effort (i.e. a balanced view of human responsibility)* (*vv. 13-16*)

    1B. The right effort is demonstrated in oral testimony. (*v. 13*)

    2B. The right effort is demonstrated in proper priorities. (*v. 14*)

    3B. The right effort is demonstrated in diligent study. (*v. 15*)

        1C. The burden of this diligent study (*v. 15a*)

        2C. The by-product of this diligent study (*v. 15b*)

    4B. The right effort is demonstrated in unwavering resolution. (*v. 16*)

        1C. The positive side of this resolution (*v. 16a*)

        2C. The negative side of this resolution (*v. 16b*)

Psalm 119

ג

Gimel

In Psalm 119 verse 17-24 the man of God's prayers for Divine intervention are ignited by two painful contrasts.

1A. His prayers for relief are ignited by a painful contrast between
  his anticipation and the apathy of his enemies. (vv. 17-21)
     1B. He voices the prayers for relief. *(vv. 17-19)*
        1C. He prays generally for personal intervention. *(v. 17)*
        2C. He prays specifically for propositional intervention: *(vv. 18-19)*
           1D. First he phrases his request positively. *(v. 18)*
           2D. Then he phrases his request negatively. *(v. 19)*
     2B. He voices the painful contrast between: *(vv. 20-21)*
        1C. how his anticipation draws him to God's Word *(v. 20)*
        2C. how his enemies' apathy repels them from God's Word *(v. 21)*
2A. His prayer for respect is ignited by a painful contrast between
  the slander of his enemies and his satisfaction. (vv. 22-24)
     1B. He voices the prayer for respect. *(v. 22)*
     2B. He voices the painful contrast between: *(vv. 23-24)*
        1C. how his enemies have slandered him *(v. 23a)*
        2C. how God's Word has satisfied him *(vv. 23b-24)*

Psalm 119

ד

Daleth

In verses 25–32 of Psalm 119 the man of God voices two complaints which become the occasions for his requests and professions concerning character and conduct.

1A. The first complaint takes in verses 25-27 and may be paraphrased: *"I am utterly humiliated!" (vv. 25-27)*

    1B. His humiliation leads to the vocalization of this complaint. *(v. 25a)*

    2B. His humiliation also leads into his requests and professions. *(vv. 25b-27)*

        1C. His general request for spiritual revitalization *(v. 25b)*

        2C. His specific requests and professions concerning edification *(vv. 26-27)*

            1D. They are based upon past edification. *(v. 26)*

            2D. They are based upon the hope for future edification. *(v. 27)*

2A. The second complaint takes in verses 28-32 and may be paraphrased: *"I am in great anguish!" (vv. 28-32)*

    1B. His great anguish leads to the vocalization of this complaint. *(v. 28a)*

    2B. His great anguish also leads into his requests and professions. *(vv. 28b-32)*

        1C. His general request for spiritual reinforcement *(v. 28b)*

        2C. His specific requests and professions concerning integrity of life *(vv. 29-32)*

            1D. Integrity of life is based upon God's continued intervention. *(v. 29)*

                1E. The negative dimension of His intervention *(v. 29a)*

                2E. The positive dimension of His intervention *(v. 29b)*

            2D. Integrity of life is based upon an acute awareness of human responsibility: *(vv. 30-31a)*

                1E. The psalmist has decided to follow the true course of life. *(v. 30a)*

                2E. The psalmist has personally ratified God's standards. *(v. 30b)*

                3E. The psalmist has adhered to God's revelation. *(v. 31a)*

3D. Integrity of life is based upon determination being tapped into God's resources. *(vv. 31b-32)*

    1E. The prerequisite for determination: dependence *(v. 31b)*

    2E. The promise of determination: desire *(v. 32a)*

    3E. The provision for determination: dynamic *(v. 32b)*

Psalm 119

ה

He

In the fifth stanza of Psalm 119 the disciple's dependent requests enlist two levels of Divine guidance.

1A. The first level of *immediate guidance* is reflected by: *(vv. 33-35)*
   1B. his request for spiritual education *(v. 33)*
      1C. Its demand *(v. 33a)*
      2C. Its design *(v. 33b)*
   2B. his request for spiritual illumination *(v. 34)*
      1C. Its burden *(v. 34a)*
      2C. Its bearing *(v. 34b, c)*
   3B. his request for spiritual conformity *(v. 35)*
      1C. Its sanction *(v. 35a)*
      2C. Its satisfaction *(v. 35b)*
2A. The second level of *mediate guidance* is reflected by: *(vv. 36-40)*
   1B. his specific requests: *(vv. 36-37)*
      1C. his request for an affinity to God's Word instead of greediness *(v. 36)*
      2C. his request for godliness instead of emptiness *(v. 37)*
   2B. his general requests: *(vv. 38-40)*
      1C. his request for ratification *(v. 38)*
      2C. his request for relief *(v. 39)*
      3C. his request for revival *(v. 40)*

Psalm 119

ו

Waw

The child of God, being burdened by a desire for a bold testimony in Psalm 119:41–48, documents two supplications for Divine intervention with consequences and commitments.

1A. A positively expressed supplication for *grace for communication (vv. 41-42)*
    1B. His desire *(v. 41)*
    2B. His documentation: *(v. 42)*
        1C. the anticipated consequence *(v. 42a)*
        2C. the accompanying commitment *(v. 42b)*
2A. A negatively expressed supplication for *grace for credibility (vv. 43-48)*
    1B. His desire *(v. 43a)*
    2B. His documentation: *(vv. 43b-48)*
        1C. the anticipated consequences: *(vv. 44, 45a, 46-48)*
            1D. obedience *(v. 44)*
            2D. freedom *(v. 45a)*
            3D. boldness *(v. 46)*
            4D. satisfaction: *(vv. 47–48)*
                1E. its emotional manifestation *(v. 47)*
                2E. its volitional manifestation *(v. 48a)*
                3E. its rational manifestation *(v. 48b)*
        2C. the accompanying commitments: *(vv. 43b, 45b)*
            1D. his expectation of God's Word *(v. 43b)*
            2D. his exploration in God's Word *(v. 45b)*

Psalm 119

ז

Zayin

Amidst life's tough realities three cycles of remembrance provide spiritual perspective for the child of God.

1A. Cycle 1: amidst his affliction *he anticipates God's remembrance* and obtains comfort. *(vv. 49-50)*

    1B. The remembrance: his future expectation is grounded upon a past assurance. *(v. 49)*

    2B. The result: his present consolation is grounded upon a past precedent. *(v. 50)*

2A. Cycle 2: amidst his adversity *he remembers the Word of God* and feels righteous indignation *(i.e. towards the apostates). (vv. 51-53)*

    1B. The reality: their hostility contrasts with his integrity. *(v. 51)*

    2B. The remembrance: the Word's fidelity supplies his consolation. *(v. 52)*

    3B. The result: his indignation stems from their apostasy. *(v. 53)*

3A. Cycle 3: amidst his alienation *he remembers the God of the Word* and matures in obedience. *(vv. 54-56)*

    1B. The reality: God's Word pre-empts his loneliness. *(v. 54)*

    2B. The remembrance: God's Person prompts his commitment. *(v. 55)*

    3B. The result: God's providence pilots his sanctification. *(v. 56)*

Psalm 119

Heth

As we gain some insight into the psalmist's thinking, three moods surface from the various contexts undergirding his promises and petitions in verses 57–64.

1A. A mood of *compensation* surfaces out of a context of providence. *(vv. 57-60)*
    1B. His recognition of this compensation *(v. 57a)*
    2B. His reaction to this compensation *(v. 58)*
    3B. His responsibilities in view of this compensation: *(vv. 57b, 59-60)*
        1C. commitment *(v. 57b)*
        2C. contemplation *(v. 59a)*
        3C. commencement *(vv. 59b-60)*
2A. A mood of *consternation* surfaces out of a context of persecution. *(vv. 61-62)*
    1B. his recognition of this consternation *(v. 61a)*
    2B. his reaction to this consternation *(v. 61b)*
    3B. his responsibility in spite of this consternation *(v. 62)*
3A. A mood of *continuation* surfaces out of a context of privilege. *(vv. 63-64)*
    1B. His reasoning leading to the recognition of this continuation: *(vv. 63-64a)*
        1C. in its micro setting of true community *(v. 63)*
        2C. in its macro setting of all creation *(v. 64a)*
    2B. His responsibility commensurate with this continuation *(v. 64b)*

Psalm 119

ט

Teth

In verses 65–72, we find the child of God painting three pictures of Divine goodness on a dark canvas of human distress.

1A. The first picture is one of a ***past restoration*** to fellowship by means of distress. *(vv. 65-67)*

    1B. The man of God's appraisal of his restoration to fellowship *(v. 65)*

    2B. The man of God's prayer since his restoration to fellowship *(v. 66)*

    3B. The man of God's confession about his restoration to fellowship *(v. 67)*

        1C. His confession about the past *(v. 67a)*

        2C. His confession about the present *(v. 67b)*

2A. The second picture is one of a ***present preservation*** in the midst of distress. *(vv. 68-70)*

    1B. The man of God's preservation depends upon God's Person and provision. *(v. 68)*

    2B. The man of God's preservation depends upon his reliance upon God's Word. *(vv. 69-70)*

        1C. He must rely on the Word because of the action of wicked men. *(v. 69)*

        2C. He must rely on the Word because of the nature of wicked men. *(v. 70)*

3A. The third picture is one of ***continued edification*** as the product of distress. *(vv. 71-72)*

    1B. God uses the man of God's distress to catalyze spiritual progress. *(v. 71)*

    2B. God uses the man of God's distress to cultivate spiritual priorities. *(v. 72)*

Psalm 119

ﬧ

Yodh

In the tenth stanza of Psalm 119, the man of God echoes four concentric circles of prayer requests based upon his chronic experience with affliction.

1A. The largest circle encompasses *the man of God's desire for deep maturity.* *(vv. 73, 80)*

    1B. His desire leads him to pray for more discernment of the Word of God. *(v. 73)*

        1C. The predication of his prayer *(v. 73a)*

        2C. The proposal of his prayer *(v. 73b)*

        3C. The purpose of his prayer *(v. 73c)*

    2B. His desire leads him to pray for total conformity to the Word of God. *(v. 80)*

        1C. The request for conformity *(v. 80a)*

        2C. The reason for conformity *(v. 80b)*

2A. The second largest circle encompasses *the man of God's concern for other believers.* *(vv. 74, 79)*

    1B. He prays to be a visual testimony to other believers. *(v. 74)*

    2B. He prays to be a vocal testimony to other believers. *(v. 79)*

3A. The third largest circle encompasses *the man of God's exposure to trials.* *(vv. 75, 78)*

    1B. The man of God's acknowledgement of the Divine Source of trials *(v. 75)*

    2B. The man of God's petition concerning the human instruments of trials *(v. 78)*

4A. The innermost circle encompasses *the man of God's deepest needs.* *(vv. 76-77)*

    1B. His need for Divine consolation *(v. 76)*

    2B. His need for Divine compassion *(v. 77)*

Psalm 119

כ

Kaph

Two crescendos of lament in verses 119:81–88 drive the desperate disciple to an unreserved dependence upon God and His resources.

1A. The first crescendo issues primarily from *a theological context*
   (i.e. God and the psalmist). (vv. 81-84)
   1B. He voices his personal predicament: *(vv. 81-82)*
      1C. by exposing his feelings *(vv. 81-82a)*
      2C. by expressing his frustration *(v. 82b)*
   2B. He voices his precarious perseverance by employing a vivid metaphor
      of contrast. *(v. 83)*
   3B. He voices his dependent pleas by surfacing the depths
      of his exasperation. *(v. 84)*
      1C. His transparent plea *(v. 84a)*
      2C. His transitional plea *(v. 84b)*
2A. The second crescendo issues primarily from *a sociological context*
   (i.e. God, the psalmist, and his enemies). (vv. 85-88)
   1B. He voices his painful predicament: *(vv. 85-86)*
      1C. by exposing their tactics *(v. 85)*
      2C. by extolling God's truth *(v. 86a)*
      3C. by expressing his turmoil *(v. 86b)*
   2B. He voices his precarious perseverance by contrasting their determination
      and his dedication. *(v. 87)*
   3B. He voices his dependent plea: *(v. 88)*
      1C. by appealing to precedent *(v. 88a)*
      2C. by adding a promise *(v. 88b)*

Psalm 119

ל

Lamedh

Within this grand stanza we find two consistencies upon which the child of God may always depend.

1A. *The stability of God and revelation (vv. 89-91)*
   1B. His special revelation is stable. *(v. 89)*
      1C. The focal-point of this stability *(v. 89a)*
      2C. The firmness of this stability *(v. 89b)*
   2B. His personal revelation is stable. *(v. 90a)*
   3B. His general revelation is stable: *(vv. 90b-91)*
      1C. via creation *(v. 90b)*
      2C. via preservation *(v. 90c-91)*
2A. *The sufficiency of God's special revelation (i.e. His Word) (vv. 92-96)*
   1B. This sufficiency includes all areas of faith and practice. *(vv. 92-94)*
      1C. The Word's sufficiency in testimony *(v. 92)*
      2C. The Word's sufficiency in salvation: *(vv. 93-94)*
         1D. considered historically *(v. 93)*
         2D. considered progressively *(v. 94)*
   2B. This sufficiency meets attacks from the world. *(v. 95)*
      1C. The reality of them *(v. 95a)*
      2C. The relief from them *(v. 95b)*
   3B. This sufficiency transcends human limitations. *(v. 96)*
      1C. The limitation of the finite *(v. 96a)*
      2C. The liberation of the infinite *(v. 96b)*

Psalm 119

מ

Mem

Two exclamations form the framework of the disciple's gratitude for Divine wisdom in verses 97–104.

1A. The *introductory exclamation* concerning Divine wisdom *(vv. 97-102)*

    1B. The special adoration of this Divine wisdom *(v. 97)*

        1C. The confession of it *(v. 97a)*

        2C. The confirmation of it *(v. 97b)*

    2B. The special advantages of this Divine wisdom *(vv. 98-102)*

        1C. It gives prudence in the presence of antagonists. *(v. 98)*

        2C. It multiplies insight in the presence of intellectuals. *(v. 99)*

        3C. It increases discernment in the presence of the more experienced. *(v. 100)*

        4C. It grants direction in the presence of alternatives. *(vv. 101-102)*

            1D. This direction is viewed from the positive *(i.e., preventative)* perspective. *(v. 101)*

            2D. This direction is viewed from the negative *(i.e., prohibitive)* perspective. *(v. 102)*

2A. The *summary exclamation* concerning Divine wisdom *(vv. 103-104)*

    1B. The summary association of this Divine wisdom: the satisfaction of honey *(v. 103)*

    2B. The summary advantage of this Divine wisdom: the suppression of sin *(v. 104)*

Psalm 119

נ

In considering verses 105 through 112, three settings form the background for the man of God's resolutions to obedience.

1A. *A positive setting of guidance* is the basis for this resolution to obedience. *(vv. 105-106)*

    1B. The man of God's testimony concerning the guidance of the Word of God *(v. 105)*

        1C. It guides in the next immediate step of life. *(v. 105a)*

        2C. It guides throughout the whole journey of life. *(v. 105b)*

    2B. The man of God's resolution in view of this guidance from the Word of God *(v. 106)*

2A. *A negative setting of distress* is the basis for these resolutions to obedience. *(vv. 107-110)*

    1B. The man of God's distress encourages him to depend upon his LORD. *(vv. 107-108)*

        1C. He depends upon his LORD to enliven him. *(v. 107)*

        2C. He depends upon his LORD to enlighten him. *(v. 108)*

    2B. The man of God's distress emboldens him to make resolutions. *(vv. 109-110)*

        1C. He resolves fidelity to God's Word in the face of his ever-present dangers. *(v. 109)*

        2C. He resolves conformity to God's Word in the face of his seemingly eventual demise. *(v. 110)*

3A. *A positive setting of contentment* is the basis for this resolution to obedience. *(vv. 111-112)*

    1B. The man of God's contentment is a motivational reality. *(v. 111)*

        1C. He is content because the Word of God is his eternal inheritance. *(v. 111a)*

        2C. He is content because the Word of God is his present satisfaction. *(v. 111b)*

    2B. The man of God's contentment leads him to a faithful practice of God's Word. *(v. 112)*

Psalm 119

ס

In Psalm 119:113–120 the child of God passionately deals with three critical areas in his life.

1A. He deals with his *critical emotions. (vv. 113, 120)*
    1B. He reveals his aggravation towards the hypocritical. *(v. 113a)*
    2B. He reacts with his ardor for the Bible. *(v. 113b)*
    3B. He reflects upon his awe of: *(v. 120)*
        1C. the God of the Word *(v. 120a)*
        2C. the Word of God *(v. 120b)*
2A. He deals with his *critical relationships. (vv. 114-115; 118-119)*
    1B. The relationship between God and himself provides security in life. *(v. 114)*
    2B. The relationship between his enemies and himself provokes resolution for life. *(v. 115)*
    3B. The relationship between God, his enemies, and himself promotes perspective on life: *(vv. 118–119)*
        1C. God is in control of apostates. *(v. 118)*
        2C. God is in control of autocrats. *(v. 119)*
3A. He deals with his *critical needs. (vv. 116-117)*
    1B. He is desperately in need of God's assurance. *(v. 116)*
        1C. The declarations of this need of assurance *(v. 116a, c)*
        2C. The design of this need of assurance *(v. 116b)*
    2B. He is desperately in need of God's assistance. *(v. 117)*
        1C. The declaration of this need of assistance *(v. 117a)*
        2C. The designs of this need of assistance *(v. 117b, c)*

Psalm 119

ע

Ayin

Three personal affirmations provide the framework for the disciple's bold requests for Divine attention in Psalm 119:121–128.

1A. His *ethical* affirmation *(vv. 121-122)*
    1B. Its expression *(v. 121a)*
    2B. Its expectations: *(vv. 121b-122)*
        1C. prevention *(vv. 121b, 122b)*
        2C. protection *(v. 122a)*
2A. His *devotional* affirmation *(vv. 123-124)*
    1B. Its expression *(v. 123)*
    2B. Its expectations: *(v. 124)*
        1C. grace *(v. 124a)*
        2C. guidance *(v. 124b)*
3A. His *relational* affirmation *(vv. 125-128)*
    1B. Its expression *(v. 125a)*
    2B. Its expectations: *(vv. 125b-128)*
        1C. These expectations are voiced: *(vv. 125b-126a)*
            1D. illumination *(v. 125b, c)*
            2D. intervention *(v. 126a)*
        2C. These expectations are verified: *(vv. 126b–128)*
            1D. negatively, by the actions of the oppressors *(v. 126b)*
            2D. positively, by the attitudes of the oppressed; e.g.: *(vv. 127-128)*
                1E. loving what is right *(vv. 127-128a)*
                2E. loathing what is wrong *(v. 128b)*

Psalm 119

פ

Pe

In this seventeenth stanza of Psalm 119 the child of God contemplates Divine direction from the context of two different associations.

1A. The child of God contemplates Divine direction through *a positive association* with the obedient. *(vv. 129-132)*

    1B. The statements of the child of God in association with the obedient *(vv. 129-131)*

        1C. His statement on the extraordinary nature of revelation *(v. 129)*

        2C. His statement on the value of illumination *(v. 130)*

        3C. His statement on strong desire for spiritual refreshment *(v. 131)*

    2B. The privileges available to the child of God in association with the obedient *(v. 132)*

2A. The child of God contemplates Divine direction through *a negative association* with the disobedient. *(vv. 133-136)*

    1B. The needs of the child of God in association with the disobedient *(vv. 133-135)*

        1C. His need for stability *(v. 133)*

        2C. His need for rescue *(v. 134)*

        3C. His need for communion *(v. 135)*

    2B. The burden of the child of God in association with the disobedient *(v. 136)*

        1C. The effect of his burden *(v. 136a)*

        2C. The reason for his burden *(v. 136b)*

Psalm 119

צ

Tsadhe

Verses 137–144 deal with three adverse situations from which the child of God extols the fidelity of God and His Word.

1A. The first adverse situation is that *he is surrounded by infidels.* *(vv. 137-139)*

    1B. The resources of Divine fidelity *(vv. 137-138)*

        1C. The fidelity of God's Person. *(v. 137a)*

        2C. The fidelity of God's Propositions *(vv. 137b-138)*

    2B. The reality of human infidelity *(v. 139)*

2A. The second adverse situation is that *he is rejected by others.* *(vv. 140-141)*

    1B. His rejection is compensated for by God's refined revelation. *(v. 140)*

    2B. His rejection does not affect his obedience. *(v. 141)*

3A. The third adverse situation is that *he is besieged by pressure and stress.* *(vv. 142-144)*

    1B. The weapons enabling him to withstand pressure and stress *(v. 142)*

    2B. The warfare against pressure and stress *(vv. 143-144)*

        1C. He knows how to experience joy in the midst of pressure and stress. *(v. 143)*

        2C. He prays for Divine enablement in the face of pressure and stress. *(v. 144)*

Psalm 119

ק

Qoph

As one moves through Psalm 119:145-152 it should become obvious that the disciple's two choruses of lamentation gradually ebb in the light of Divine sufficiencies.

1A. The disciple's *cries for protection* result in his being drawn to the Word of God. *(vv. 145-148)*

    1B. His cries for protection express his need for dependency. *(vv. 145-146)*

        1C. God needs to respond in order for him to live obediently. *(v. 145)*

        2C. God needs to rescue in order for him to live obediently. *(v. 146)*

    2B. His acknowledged dependency leads to an anticipation of God's sufficiencies. *(vv. 147-148)*

        1C. Early in the morning he anticipates God's good response through His Word. *(v. 147)*

        2C. Late at night he appropriates God's good response through His Word. *(v. 148)*

2A. The disciple's *cries for attention* rest in his being drawn to the God of the Word. *(vv. 149-152)*

    1B. His cries for attention express his need for a sustaining relationship. *(v. 149)*

    2B. His need for a sustaining relationship is satisfied through a renewed appreciation of God's sufficiencies. *(vv. 150-152)*

        1C. This appreciation is intensified by contrast. *(v. 150)*

        2C. This appreciation is implemented by contact. *(v. 151)*

        3C. This appreciation is integrated by confidence. *(v. 152)*

Psalm 119

ר

Resh

The disciple's three cycles of cries for deliverance in verses 153–160 progressively subside in the presence of the comforting attributes and assurances of God and His Word.

1A. The *emotional cycle* of cries is related to the psalmist's affliction. *(vv. 153-54)*
    1B. This emotional cycle comes through cries which refer to his affliction explicitly. *(v. 153)*
    2B. This emotional cycle also comes through cries which refer to his affliction implicitly. *(v. 154)*
2A. The *theological cycle* of cries is related to the psalmist's afflicters. *(vv. 155-58)*
    1B. The comprehensive theological assertion about his afflicters *(i.e. a soteriological assertion) (v. 155)*
    2B. The comparative theological assertion about his afflicters *(i.e. a providential assertion): (vv. 156-57)*
        1C. the light side of this comparison: abounding grace *(v. 156)*
        2C. the dark side of this comparison: abounding grief *(v. 157)*
    3B. The critical theological assertion about his afflicters *(i.e. a hamartiological assertion) (v. 158)*
3A. The *tranquil cycle* of cries is related to the psalmist's affection. *(vv. 159-60)*
    1B. This tranquil cycle is reflected in the statement of his affection. *(v. 159)*
    2B. This tranquil cycle is also reflected in the substructure of his affection. *(v. 160)*

Psalm 119

ש

Shin

In putting the pieces of Psalm 119:161–168 together, the reader should observe the child of God verbally laying out before the LORD six indications of basic integrity for the purpose of documenting his previous and forthcoming requests.

1A. His *godly fear* prevails over human pressure. *(v. 161)*

2A. His *godly contentment* rivals human materialism. *(v. 162)*

3A. His *godly commitment* provides perspective on human injustice. *(v. 163)*

4A. His *godly praise* is the product of Divine justice. *(v. 164)*

5A. His *godly peace (i.e. as a member of the community of the faithful)* promises a reassuring stability. *(v. 165)*

6A. His *godly obedience* is prompted by: *(vv. 166-168)*

    1B. a confident expectation *(v. 166)*

    2B. a consuming adoration *(v. 167)*

    3B. a complete penetration *(v. 168)*

Psalm 119

Taw

Two tides of petition in the final stanza of Psalm 119 recapitulate the disciple's dependence upon God and His Word.

1A. The swelling tide rises heavenward in *anticipation of communication with God.* *(vv. 169-172)*

    1B. The acute communication of his burdens *(vv. 169-170)*

        1C. His burden for scriptural insight *(v. 169)*

        2C. His burden for supernatural intervention *(v. 170)*

    2B. The accompanying communication of his blessings: *(vv. 171-172)*

        1C. personal instruction *(v. 171)*

        2C. propositional integrity *(v. 172)*

2A. The ebbing tide returns earthward in *anticipation of compassion from God.* *(vv. 173-176)*

    1B. The anticipated compassion of Divine protection *(vv. 173-174)*

        1C. The disciple's desire *(v. 173a)*

        2C. The disciple's documentation *(positive) (vv. 173b-174)*

    2B. The anticipated compassion of Divine preservation *(vv. 175-176)*

        1C. The disciple's desire *(v. 175)*

        2C. The disciple's documentation *(negative and positive) (vv. 176)*

Psalm 119

A commentary on all of Psalm 119 by this author is available at *Wipf & Stock, Publisher.*

Phone: 541-344-11528 Fax: 541-344-1506 www.wiphandstock.com email: order@wipfandstock.com

Psalm 120

In Psalm 120, one of the LORD's pressured pilgrims brings up (seemingly in reverse order) two realities which characterize a believer's dependent existence in the context of a hostile world.

1A. The reality of *his prayers to God (vv. 1-4)*
    1B. His past prayers *(v. 1)*
    2B. His present prayers: *(vv. 2-4)*
        1C. for rescue *(v. 2)*
        2C. for retribution *(vv. 3-4)*
            1D. This desired retribution is poetically applied. *(v. 3)*
            2D. This desired retribution is penally appropriate. *(v. 4)*
2A. The reality of *his problems in the world (vv. 5-7)*
    1B. The hostility of his "neighborhood": *(v. 5-6)*
        1C. geographically exemplified *(v. 5)*
        2C. ethically exposed *(v. 6)*
    2B. The frustration of his "neighboring" *(v. 7)*
        1C. He stands for peace. *(v. 7a)*
        2C. They strive for war. *(v. 7b)*

Psalm 121

In Psalm 121 the pilgrim shares how he comforted himself in the LORD by sharpening his spiritual vision, then he crafts for us two prescription lenses by which we also might see more clearly the merciful care of God.

1A. Through his lens of affirmation he would have us perceive
the wonder of God's care. (vv. 1-2)

   1B. His question contemplates the wonder of God's care. *(v. 1)*

   2B. His answer confirms the wonder of God's care. *(v. 2)*

2A. Through his lens of application he would have us ponder
the workings of God's care. (vv. 3-8)

   1B. He wants us to focus with him on the community
   of God's care. *(vv. 3-4)*

      1C. with an individual application *(v. 3)*

      2C. with a corporate application *(v. 4)*

   2B. He also wants us to focus with him on the comfort
   of God's care. *(vv. 5-6)*

      1C. The application of this comfort *(v. 5a)*

      2C. Some illustrations of this comfort *(vv. 5b-6)*

   3B. He finally wants us to focus with him on the comprehensiveness
   of God's care. *(vv. 7-8)*

      1C. The panoramic view of the comprehensiveness of God's care *(v. 7)*

      2C. The linear view of the comprehensiveness of God's care *(v. 8)*

Psalm 122

Psalm 122 provides us with three insights into the passion of the pilgrim-poet as he pays tribute to Jerusalem, the special city of God.

1A. In verses 1-2 we gain insight into
    his excitement over visiting the city of God. (vv. 1-2)
        1B. He was always excited about going there. *(v. 1)*
        2B. He was always excited about being there. *(v. 2)*
2A. In verses 3-5 we gain insight into
    his historical reflections about the city of God. (vv. 3-5)
        1B. The compactness of construction *(v. 3)*
        2B. The designated place for praise *(v. 4)*
        3B. The historical center of administration *(v. 5)*
3A. In verses 6-9 we gain insight into
    his desires for continuing blessings in connection with the city of God. (vv. 6-9)
        1B. The expressions of his desires: *(vv. 6-7)*
            1C. through an exhortation to the community *(v. 6a)*
            2C. through examples in the presence of the community *(vv. 6b-7)*
        2B. The explanations of his desires: *(vv. 8-9)*
            1C. They are based upon the unity of the community.
            (v. 8)
            2C. They are based upon the sanctity of the community's worship center.
            (v. 9)

Psalm 123

Psalm 123 is a biblical opera consisting of three acts which tell a story of straining faith under heavy fire.

1A. Act one develops the theme of *submissive patience. (vv. 1-2)*
    1B. It opens with an aria. *(v. 1)*
    2B. It responds with an antiphonal chorus. *(v. 2)*
2A. Act two develops the theme of *sustained prayer. (v. 3a)*
3A. Act three develops the theme of *severe persecution. (vv. 3b-4)*

Psalm 124

Psalm 124 is a refresher course on Divine protection taught in two poetic installments.

1A. The first installment is dedicated to *the community's reflections. (vv. 1-5)*
    1B. The "if" part of these reflections recalls the mercy of God. *(vv. 1-2)*
    2B. The "then" part of these reflections recalls the meanness of men. *(vv. 3-5)*
        1C. Men wanted to devour them. *(v. 3)*
        2C. Men wanted to drown them. *(vv. 4-5)*
2A. The second installment is dedicated to *the community's responses. (vv. 6-8)*
    1B. Their response of reverence *(vv. 6-7)*
        1C. Its expression *(v. 6a)*
        2C. Its expansion *(vv. 6b-7)*
    2B. Their response of recognition *(v. 8)*

Psalm 125

"White? Black? (or, Gray?)"

In Psalm 125 the poet probes the whole theocratic community reminding them about the two divinely determined categories into which all professing religionists fall. In so doing, he also issues a warning to spiritual fence-walkers.

1A. The category of *those who adhere to Yahweh (vv. 1-4)*

    1B. His probings: *(vv. 1-3)*

        1C. He probes by characterizing those who belong to this category. *(vv. 1-2)*

        2C. He probes by contrasting those who might not belong to this category. *(v. 3)*

    2B. His prayer *(v. 4)*

2A. The category of *those who apostatize from Yahweh (v. 5)*

    1B. His probings: *(v. 5a, b)*

        1C. He probes by characterizing those who belong to this category. *(v. 5a)*

        2C. He probes by casting them in with all the condemned. *(v. 5b)*

    2B. His prayer *(v. 5c)*

Note that by contextual implication his prayer is for the true Israelites of his theocratic community (cf., e.g., Rom. 2:29, Rom. 9:6b and Gal. 6:16 in the NT).

Psalm 126

"The Back to the Future Psalm"

Standing on the shaky ground of his historical present, the psalmist casts two glances at the restoration of Jews to the land.

1A. *His glance backward in time* attests to the gladness of a past restoration. *(vv. 1-3)*

    1B. Its accomplished fact *(v. 1)*

    2B. Its attendant features: *(vv. 2-3)*

        1C. Celebrations *(v. 2a, b)*

        2C. Contemplations *(vv. 2c-3a)*

            1D. From without *(v. 2c d)*

            2D. From within *(v. 3a)*

        3C. Contentment *(v. 3b)*

2A. *His glance forward in time* anticipates the hope of a future restoration. *(vv. 4-6)*

    1B. His prayer for it *(v. 4)*

    2B. His picture of it: *(vv. 5-6)*

        1C. sketched out *(v. 5)*

        2C. filled in *(v. 6)*

Psalm 127

The psalmist shares with us two secrets to true success in a hostile world.

1A. The first secret is that *human pursuits must be brought into balance* by a clear recognition of Divine providence. *(vv. 1-2)*

    1B. This secret holds true for the pursuit of shelter. *(v. 1a, b)*

    2B. This secret holds true for the pursuit of security. *(v. 1c, d)*

    3B. This secret holds true for the pursuit of sustenance. *(v. 2)*

2A. The second secret is that *human prestige and power must be brought into balance* by a clear recognition of Divine provision. *(vv. 3-5)*

    1B. This secret is affirmed. *(v. 3)*

    2B. This secret is appreciated: *(vv. 4-5)*

        1C. from an ancient near eastern military perspective *(vv. 4-5a)*

        2C. from an ancient near eastern judicial perspective *(v. 5b, c)*

Psalm 128

This psalm contains two proclamations of divine blessing upon a person who truly obeys the LORD.

1A. The first proclamation emphasizes *productivity*. *(vv. 1-3)*

    1B. Its expression *(v. 1)*

    2B. Its examples: *(vv. 2-3)*

        1C. Your food will be satisfying. *(v. 2)*

        2C. Your family will be satisfying. *(v. 3)*

2A. The second proclamation emphasizes *longevity*. *(vv. 4-6)*

    1B. Its expression *(v. 4)*

    2B. Its examples: *(vv. 5-6)*

        1C. You will enjoy your grand city. *(v. 5)*

        2C. You will enjoy your grandchildren. *(v. 6)*

Psalm 129

The community's two interrelated contemplations in Psalm 129 illustrate how God's people can have confidence in crises.

1A. Their contemplation about *past help* *(vv. 1-4)*

    1B. This past help is contemplated from the vantage point of secular history. *(vv. 1-2)*

        1C. They had often been knocked down. *(vv. 1-2a)*

        2C. Nevertheless, they had never been knocked out. *(v. 2b)*

    2B. This past help is more importantly contemplated from the vantage point of salvation history *(vv. 3-4)*

        1C. Their adversaries were mean. *(v. 3)*

        2C. Their Advocate was merciful. *(v. 4)*

2A. Their contemplation about *future hope* *(vv. 5-8)*

    1B. Such future hope is contemplated categorically. *(v. 5)*

        1C. The scope of their adversaries *(v. 5a)*

        2C. The shaming of their adversaries *(v. 5b)*

    2B. Such future hope is also contemplated illustratively. *(vv. 6-8)*

        1C. Their adversaries will not be productive. *(vv. 6-7)*

        2C. Their adversaries will not be popular. *(v. 8)*

Psalm 130

Nearly overwhelmed with the realities of human sin and divine salvation, the psalmist wrestles with these issues in two adjacent arenas.

1A. He first wrestles with them in the *personal arena. (vv. 1-6)*
    1B. His personal prayers suggest that he has been wrestling with these realities. *(vv. 1-2)*
    2B. His personal ponderings state that he indeed is wrestling with these realities. *(vv. 3-4)*
        1C. The weight of human sin *(v. 3)*
        2C. The wonder of divine salvation *(v. 4)*
    3B. His personal patience supports what he is learning by wrestling with these realities. *(vv. 5-6)*
2A. He finally wrestles with them in the *corporate arena. (vv. 7-8)*
    1B. His burden suggests that his community needed to learn what he had been learning about these realities. *(v. 7a)*
    2B. His bases support that his community needed to ponder what he had been pondering about these realities. *(vv. 7b-8)*
        1C. They needed to ponder God's grace. *(v. 7b, c)*
        2C. They needed to ponder God's mercy. *(v. 8)*

Psalm 131

In Psalm 131 we are able to gain some insight into two stages of the psalmist's life as he grew and developed spiritually.

1A. His *maturing* stage *(vv. 1-2)*
    1B. Its products *(v. 1)*
        1C. A humility of "heart"
        2C. A humility of "eyes"
        3C. A humility of ambition and accomplishment
    2B. Its process *(v. 2)*
        1C. Indicated *(v. 2a)*
        2C. Illustrated: *(v. 2b, c)*
            1D. the analogy *(v. 2b)*
            2D. its application *(v. 2c)*
2A. His *mentoring* stage *(v. 3)*
    1B. His audience
    2B. His advice
        1C. Its demand
        2C. Its duration

Psalm 132

Psalm 132 is a complex royal song of Zion that broadcasts its burdens to us from two echo chambers.

1A. From its secondary echo chamber come *dependent prayers and earnest resolves.* *(vv. 1-10)*

    1B. The psalmist prays for the LORD to respond. *(vv. 1-7)*

        1C. The voicing of his prayer *(v. 1)*

        2C. The vindication of his prayer *(vv. 2-7)*

            1D. David's personal resolves *(vv. 1b-5)*

            2D. The people's resolves *(vv. 6-7)*

    2B. The psalmist prays for the LORD to reside. *(vv. 8-10)*

        1C. The voicing of his prayer *(vv. 8-9)*

        2C. The vindication of his prayer *(v. 10)*

2A. From its primary echo chamber come *Divine promises and effectual resolves.* *(vv. 11-18)*

    1B. The identification of these Divine promises and resolves. *(vv. 11-16)*

        1C. The royal ones *(vv. 11-12)*

        2C. The residence ones *(vv. 13-16)*

    2B. The integration of these Divine promises and resolves. *(vv. 17-18)*

Psalm 133

The psalmist employs two means to develop his theme about the preciousness of true fellowship.

1A. By *means of a proclamation* he introduces his theme about the preciousness of true fellowship. *(v. 1)*

2A. By *means of pictures* he illustrates his theme about the preciousness of true fellowship. *(vv. 2-3)*

    1B. His cultic picture *(v. 2)*

    2B. His geographical picture *(v. 3)*

Psalm 134

"The Privilege of Praise and the Promise of Blessing"

The movement of this liturgical psalm of blessing is like the two swings of a pendulum.

1A. As the pendulum swings in one direction, *the people urge the priestly attendants to praise the LORD. (vv. 1-2)*
  1B. The general call to praise with a focus upon the attendants *(v. 1)*
  2B. The expanded call to praise with a focus upon their activities *(v. 2)*
    1C. The accompanying gesture of praise *(v. 2a)*
    2C. The verbal acclamation of praise *(v. 2b)*
2A. As the pendulum swings in the other direction, *the priestly attendants pronounce the LORD's blessing upon the people. (v. 3)*
  1B. This blessing with a focus upon God's person and special place *(v. 3a)*
  2B. This blessing with a focus on God's power *(v. 3b)*

Psalm 135

Psalm 135 is an extended hymn of worship composed of three basic stanzas.

1A. Stanza one contains *an invocation to praise Yahweh-God. (vv. 1-3)*

    1B. An initial invocation focuses on the privilege of praise *(v. 1a,b)*

    2B. A follow-up invocation focuses on the people who are to praise *(vv. 1c-2)*

    3B. A final invocation focuses on the precedent for praise *(v. 3)*

2A. Stanza two supplies some *reasons for praising Yahweh-God. (vv. 4-18)*

    1B. His people should praise Him because of their salvation *(v. 4)*

    2B. His people should praise Him because of His supremacy: *(vv. 5-18)*

        1C. over everything in general *(vv. 5-7)*

        2C. over history in particular *(vv. 8-14)*

            1D. Both past history *(vv. 8-12)*

            2D. And current and future history *(vv. 13-14)*

        3C. over so-called deities in contrast *(vv. 15-18)*

3A. Stanza three contains *final invitations to praise Yahweh-God. (vv. 19-21)*

    1B. With an emphasis on the companies who are to praise Him *(vv. 19-20)*

        1C. The whole nation *(v. 19a)*

        2C. All the priests *(v. 19b)*

        3C. All the Levites *(v. 20a)*

        4C. All God-fearers *(v. 20b)*

    2B. With an emphasis on the center from which they are to join together to praise Him *(v. 21)*

Psalm 136

Psalm 136 contains two unequally long poetic portions which call the worshipping community to praise God for His Person and works.

1A. The longer portion reviews selected reasons for praising Him. *(vv. 1-22)*

    1B. Some selected reasons relating to His Person *(vv. 1-3)*

        1C. He is beneficent Yahweh. *(v. 1)*

        2C. He is the mighty God of gods. *(v. 2)*

        3C. He is the loyal Lord of lords. *(v. 3)*

    2B. Some selected reasons relating to His works *(vv. 4-22)*

        1C. Concerning His works in natural history *(vv. 4-9)*

            1D. Comprehensively surveyed *(v. 4)*

            2D. Specifically sampled *(vv. 5-9)*

        2C. Concerning His works in salvation history *(vv. 10-22)*

            1D. Focusing on the Exodus *(vv. 10-16)*

            2D. Focusing on the Conquest *(vv. 17-22)*

2A. *The shorter portion recaps selected reasons for praising Him. (vv. 23-26)*

    1B. A recap of His works *(vv. 23-25)*

        1C. In salvation history *(vv. 23-24)*

        2C. In natural history *(v. 25)*

    2B. A recap of His Person *(v. 26)*

CHORUS
key li-o-lam has-do

Psalm 137

Psalm 137 is a passionate song that thematically focuses on two different kinds of remembrance.

1A. It first focuses on *a human kind of remembrance of past and present pain. (vv. 1-6)*
    1B. The realities of past and present pain *(v. 1)*
    2B. The responses to past and present pain *(v. 2-6)*
        1C. The reluctance of the community *(vv. 2-4)*
            1D. This reluctance is displayed *(v. 2)*
            2D. This reluctance is documented *(v. 3)*
            3D. This reluctance is defended *(v. 4)*
        2C. The resolves of the psalmist *(vv. 5-6)*
            1D. Revealed by the self-curse of his playing ability *(v. 5)*
            2D. Revealed by the self-curse of his singing ability *(v. 6)*
2A. It finally focuses on *a divine kind of remembrance of future payback. (vv. 7-9)*
    1B. The prayer for payback *(v. 7a)*
    2B. The parties for payback *(vv. 7b-8)*
        1C. The Edomites *(v. 7b)*
        2C. The Babylonians *(v. 8)*
    3B. The precedent for payback *(i.e. both by practice and prophecy) (v. 9)*

Psalm 138

Two priorities of worship are modeled for us by this psalmist.

1A. The priority of *thanksgiving* *(vv. 1-6)*

    1B. His devotion to personal thanksgiving *(vv. 1-3)*

        1C. The expressions of his devotion *(vv. 1-2)*

        2C. The energy behind his devotion *(v. 3)*

    2B. His desire for universal thanksgiving *(vv. 4-6)*

        1C. Some calls to universal thanksgiving *(vv. 4-5a)*

        2C. Selected causes for universal thanksgiving *(vv. 5b-6)*

2A. The priority of *testimony* *(vv. 7-8)*

    1B. His direct testimony about Divine precedents *(vv. 7-8b)*

        1C. The precedent of renewal *(v. 7a)*

        2C. The precedent of rescue *(v. 7b)*

        3C. The precedent of revenge *(v. 8a)*

        4C. The precedent of reliability *(v. 8b)*

    2B. His indirect testimony through dependent prayer *(v. 8c)*

Psalm 139

"The Penetrating but Precious Presence of God"

In Psalm 139, we are blessed to view two galleries of poetic portraits of selected attributes of God.

1A. The *meditation gallery* displays some of His attributes of Being. *(vv. 1-18)*
    1B. The psalmist's arrangement of God's attributes of Being *(vv. 1-16)*
        1C. The LORD's omniscience: He knows everything.
        (vv. 1-6)
        2C. The LORD's omnipresence: Everything is in His presence.
        (vv. 7-12)
        3C. The LORD's omnipotence:
        (vv. 13-16)
            1D. displayed in production *(vv. 13-14)*
            2D. displayed in providence *(vv. 15-16)*
    2B. The psalmist's adoration of God's attributes of Being *(vv. 17-18)*
2A. The *mediation gallery* displays some of His attributes of action. *(vv. 19-24)*
    1B. The LORD as Divine Warrior and Judge will condemn the wicked.
    (vv. 19-22)
        1C. Wicked people have taken their stand against God.
        (vv. 19-20)
        2C. Consequently, the psalmist has taken his stand against them.
        (vv. 21-22)
    2B. The LORD as Heart-Knower and Judge will confirm the righteous.
    (vv. 23-24)
        1C. The psalmist submits himself to God's scrutiny. *(vv. 23-24a)*
        2C. The psalmist solicits God's shepherding. *(v. 24b)*

Psalm 140

Psalm 140 contains two echoing volleys of pleas and praises prompted by the intense persecutions the psalmist was facing.

1A. The first volley, addressed to the LORD as Divine Warrior, pertains to *the protection of the psalmist. (vv. 1-7)*

    1B. His pleas for protection *(vv. 1-5)*

        1C. Round one of these pleas for protection *(vv. 1-3)*

            1D. They are voiced. *(v. 1)*

            2D. They are verified. *(vv. 2-3)*

        2C. Round two of these pleas for protection *(vv. 4-5)*

            1D. They also are first voiced. *(v. 4a, b)*

            2D. They also are then verified. *(v. 4c-5)*

    2B. His praises for protection *(vv. 6-7)*

2A. The second volley, addressed to the LORD as the Sovereign Judge, pertains to *the prosecution of the psalmist's enemies. (vv. 8-13)*

    1B. His pleas for prosecution *(vv. 8-11)*

        1C. Pay them back for their schemings! *(v. 8)*

        2C. Pay them back for their slanderings! *(vv. 9-11)*

    2B. His praises for prosecution *(vv. 12-13)*

Psalm 141

Based upon the psalmist's crisis circumstances, Psalm 141 contains four basic categories of prayers and petitions.

1A. In category one, we find his *prayers and petitions for divine acceptance. (vv. 1-2)*
    1B. Expressed forcefully *(v. 1)*
    2B. Expressed figuratively *(v. 2)*
2A. In category two, we find his *prayers and petitions for discernment. (vv. 3-4)*
    1B. With a focus on communication *(v. 3)*
    2B. With a focus on conduct *(v. 4)*
3A. In category three, we find his *prayers and petitions for correction. (vv. 5-7)*
    1B. Correction coming at him *(v. 5a-c)*
    2B. Correction coming from him *(vv. 5d-7)*
4A. In category four, we find his *prayers and petitions for protection. (vv. 8-10)*
    1B. He affirms his dependence *(v. 8a-b)*
    2B. He articulates his desires *(v. 8c-10)*
        1C. For rescue *(vv. 8c-9)*
        2C. For retribution *(v. 10)*

Psalm 142

Two different outlooks on the part of the persecuted psalmist may be detected as he puts forth his complaints and prayers in Psalm 142.

1A. His initial outlook is more *pessimistic. (vv. 1-4)*
    1B. His cryings *(vv. 1-4a)*
        1C. He voices them loudly. *(vv. 1-2)*
        2C. He vindicates them boldly. *(vv. 3-4a)*
    2B. His conclusion: There is <u>no</u> hope! *(v. 4b-d)*
2A. His improving outlook is more **optimistic.** *(vv. 5-7)*
    1B. His cryings: *(vv. 5-7b)*
        1C. manifest a calming confidence *(v.5)*
        2C. manifest continuing concerns *(vv. 6-7b)*
            1D. About a response *(v. 6a, b)*
            2D. About a rescue *(v. 6c, d)*
            3D. About a release *(v. 7a, b)*
    2B. His conclusion: There <u>is</u> hope! *(v. 7c, d)*

Psalm 143

In Psalm 143 the severely persecuted psalmist desperately generates two waves of petition that mount up before God.

1A. The first wave of petition that he generates *solicits God's attention. (vv. 1-6)*

    1B. As this first wave starts to swell, the persecuted psalmist pleads for God's grace. *(vv. 1-2)*

    2B. As this first wave crests, the persecuted psalmist presents his case before God. *(vv. 3-4)*

    3B. As this first wave subsides, the persecuted psalmist rests in and relies on the precedents of God. *(vv. 5-6)*

2A. The second wave of petition that he generates *solicits God's action. (vv. 7-12)*

    1B. As this second wave surges forth, he longs for God's responses. *(vv. 7-8)*

    2B. As this second wave rises, he begs God's rescue. *(vv. 9-11)*

    3B. As this second wave settles down, he rests in God's reliability. *(v. 12)*

Psalm 144

Propped up by bookends of affirmations of blessings, the psalmist's prayers at the core of Psalm 144 are directed to God so that He might richly bless two generations.

The Introductory Affirmation of the LORD's Blessedness *(vv. 1-2)*

1A. The psalmist's *prayers for his current generation (of which he was leader) (vv. 3-11)*
    1B. His understanding of the need for these prayers *(vv. 3-4)*
    2B. His urgency due to the occasion of these prayers *(vv. 5-8)*
        1C. This urgency calls for the powerful presence of God. *(vv. 5-6)*
        2C. This urgency calls for the personal protection of God. *(vv. 7-8)*
    3B. His unveiling of a promise to God when He answers these prayers *(vv. 9-11)*
        1C. The praise of this promise *(v. 9)*
        2C. The promptings of this promise *(vv. 10-11)*
            1D. Providentially remembered *(v. 10)*
            2D. Personally reviewed *(v. 11)*
2A. The psalmist's *prayers for the coming generation (vv. 12-14)*
    1B. His prayers for future progeny *(v. 12)*
        1C. For sons *(v. 12a)*
        2C. For daughters *(v. 12b)*
    2B. His prayers for future productivity *(vv. 13-14)*
        1C. For the fields *(v. 13a)*
        2C. For the folds *(vv. 13b-14)*

The Concluding Affirmation of the Theocracy's Blessedness *(v. 15)*.

Psalm 145

The psalmist's passion for glorifying our great and gracious God compelled him to compose a worship masterpiece of three swelling celebrations of praise followed by a coda.

1A. *He enjoys singing solo* in his first celebration
   of praise. *(vv. 1-3)*
   1B. His personal gratitude is voiced. *(vv. 1-2)*
   2B. His preeminent grounds are verified. *(v. 3)*
2A. *He enlists the community to join him* in his second celebration
   of praise. *(vv. 4-9)*
   1B. The community's privilege of praise *(vv. 4-7)*
   2B. The community's promptings to praise *(vv. 8-9)*
3A. *He enlists all creation to join both him and the community* in his third celebration
   of praise. *(vv. 10-20)*
   1B. Their reverberations of praise *(vv. 10-12)*
   2B. Their reasons for praise *(vv. 13-20)*

Coda *(v. 21)*

Psalm 146

Between his calls to praise the LORD God, the psalmist presents two different kinds of argument for the wisdom of such worship.

His Introductory Calls to Praise *(vv. 1-2)*
    The psalmist's call to the community *(v. 1a)*
    The psalmist's call to himself *(vv. 1b-2)*
        His personal challenge *(v. 1b)*
        His personal commitment *(v. 2)*

1A. His *negative* kind of argument for worshipping the LORD God:
    The tragedy of trusting in what is powerless and transitory *(vv. 3-4)*
    1B. The statement of his negative argument *(v. 3)*
    2B. Selected support for his negative argument *(v. 4)*
2A. His *positive* kind of argument for worshipping the LORD God:
    The truth about trusting in the One who is powerful and transcendent *(vv. 5-10a)*
    1B. The statement of his positive argument *(v.5)*
    2B. Selected support for his positive argument *(vv. 6-10a)*
        1C. It is supported by God's power. *(v. 6a, b)*
        2C. It is supported by God's fidelity. *(v. 6c)*
        3C. It is supported by God's justice: *(vv. 7-9)*
            1D. with application to the needy *(vv. 7-9a)*
            2D. with application to the naughty *(v. 9b)*
        4C. It is supported by God's kingship. *(v. 10a)*

A Culminating Call to Praise *(v.10b)*

Psalm 147

Psalm 147 is an invitational hymn to praise the LORD made up of three choruses of alternating adorations and attestations.

Its prelude of praise *(v. 1a)*

1A. The first chorus sings of the *pleasantness of praising the God of grace and power.* *(vv. 1b-6)*

    1B. The implicit invitation to praise the God of grace and power *(v. 1b)*

    2B. Some illustrative bases for praising the God of grace and power *(vv. 2-6)*

        1C. A recent restoration *(vv. 2-3)*

        2C. Some transcendent truths *(vv. 4-5)*

        3C. A historical precedent *(v. 6)*

2A. The second chorus sings of *the propriety of praising the God of providence.* *(vv. 7-11)*

    1B. The explicit call to praise the God of providence. *(v. 7)*

    2B. The grounds for praising the God of providence *(vv. 8-11)*

        1C. Positively confirmed *(vv. 8-9)*

        2C. Negatively contrasted *(vv. 10-11)*

3A. The third and final chorus sings of *the privilege of praising the God of all provision.* *(vv. 12-20a)*

    1B. The direct summons to praise the God of all provision *(v. 12)*

    2B. Selected reasons for praising the God of all provision *(vv. 13-20a)*

        1C. He provides for the temporal welfare of His people. *(vv. 13-18)*

            1D. This truth is directly stated *(vv. 13-14)*

            2D. This truth is indirectly supported *(vv. 15-18)*

        2C. He provides for the spiritual welfare of His people. *(vv. 19-20a)*

            1D. Verified by confirmation *(v. 19)*

            2D. Verified by contrast *(v. 20a)*

Its postlude of praise *(v. 20b)*

Psalm 148

The psalmist calls the two grand choirs of the universe together to worship their Great Creator.

His invocation of praise *(v. 1a)*

1A. He first calls *the grand celestial choir* to worship. *(vv. 1b-6)*
    1B. The location of this choir *(vv. 1b, c)*
    2B. The members of this choir *(vv. 2-4)*
        1C. Personally considered *(v. 2)*
        2C. Astronomically considered *(v. 3)*
        3C. Comprehensively considered *(v. 4)*
    3B. The grounds of gratitude of this choir *(vv. 5-6)*
2A. He next calls *the grand terrestrial choir* to worship. *(vv. 7-14b)*
    1B. The location of this choir *(v. 7a)*
    2B. The members of this choir *(vv. 7b-12)*
        1C. Oceanographically considered *(v. 7b)*
        2C. Meteorologically considered *(v. 8)*
        3C. Geographically considered *(v. 9a)*
        4C. Botanically considered *(v. 9b)*
        5C. Zoologically considered *(v. 10)*
        6C. Personally considered *(vv. 11-12)*
            1D. As to power and position *(v. 11)*
            2D. As to gender and age *(v. 12)*
    3B. The grounds of gratitude of this choir *(vv. 13-14b)*
        1C. God's grandeur *(v. 13)*
        2C. God's grace *(v. 14a ,b)*

The benediction of praise *(v. 14c)*

Psalm 149

We discover two different orientations of the praises offered to Yahweh-God in Psalm 149.

An introductory call to corporate praise *(v. 1a)*

1A. The orientation of these praises is ***past based upon actual deliverances***. *(vv. 1b-4)*
    1B. The reverberations of these praises *(vv. 1b-3)*
        1C. Vocally expressed *(v. 1b, c)*
        2C. Emotionally expressed *(v. 2)*
        3C. Choreographically expressed *(v. 3a)*
        4C. Instrumentally expressed *(v. 3b)*
    2B. The reasons for these praises *(v. 4)*
        1C. The precedent of God's delight *(v. 4a)*
        2C. The precedent of God's deliverances *(v. 4b)*
2A. The orientation of these praises is ***future based upon anticipated deliverances*** *(vv. 5-9b)*.
    1B. The recitation of these praises *(vv. 5-6)*
        1C. Theologically expressed *(vv. 5-6a)*
        2C. Theocratically expressed *(v. 6b)*
    2B. The results associated with these praises *(vv. 7-9b)*
        1C. Historically anticipated *(vv. 7-8)*
        2C. Scripturally attested *(v. 9a, b)*

A concluding call to corporate praise *(v. 9c)*

Psalm 150

Psalm 150, the final song in Israel's God-breathed Hymnbook, emphasizes three elements of universal praise to Yahweh-God.

Its festive "Hallelujah!" serves as an introduction to this last hymn *(v. 1a)*

1A. *The locations of praise (v. 1b, c)*
    1B. His earthly sanctuary *(v. 1b)*
    2B. His heavenly sanctuary *(v. 1c)*
2A. *The reasons for praise (v. 2)*
    1B. The works of God *(v. 2a)*
    2B. The wonder of God *(v. 2b)*
3A. *The means of praise (vv. 3-6)*
    1B. By means of the grand orchestra *(vv. 3-5)*
    2B. By means of the grand choir *(v. 6a)*

Its final "Hallelujah!" serves as a conclusion to this last hymn *(v. 6b)*

Notice the conductor's directions to the orchestral sections: from the wind section (v. 3a) to the strings section (v. 3b) to the percussion section accompanied by dancing (v. 4a) to a blending of stringed and wind instruments (v. 4b), and finally, pulling out all the stops, back to the percussion section (v. 5).

Psalm 119
A commentary on all of Psalm 119 by this author is available at:
Wipf & Stock, Publisher.
Phone: 541-344-11528 Fax: 541-344-1506
www.wiphandstock.com
email: order@wipfandstock.com